The Entrepreneur's Guide
to Selling

**Recent Titles in
The Entrepreneur's Guide**

The Entrepreneur's Guide

CJ Rhoads, Series Editor

The Entrepreneur's Guide to Selling

Jonathan London

PRAEGER
An Imprint of ABC-CLIO, LLC

A B C ☰ C L I O

Santa Barbara, California • Denver, Colorado • Oxford, England

Library of Congress Cataloging-in-Publication Data

London, Jonathan.
    The entrepreneur's guide to selling / Jonathan London.
        p. cm. — (The entrepreneur's guide series)
    Includes index.
    ISBN 978-0-313-35918-7 (hard copy : alk. paper) — ISBN 978-0-313-35919-4 (ebook)
1. Selling. 2. Customer relations. 3. Entrepreneurship. I. Title.
    HF5438.25.L66   2009
    658.85—dc22   2009005380

13 12 11 10 9 1 2 3 4 5

This book is also available on the World Wide Web as an eBook.

Visit www.abc-clio.com for details.

ABC-CLIO, LLC
130 Cremona Drive, P.O. Box 1911
Santa Barbara, California 93116-1911

This book is printed on acid-free paper ∞

Manufactured in the United States of America

Contents

Illustrations

TABLES

FIGURES

Acknowledgments

Bill McPherson was the first person to hire me at Olivetti. I don't know why he did, but he saw something in me and gave me the chance to be a salesperson.

I want to thank Dennis Chambers for referring me to Jeff Olson at Praeger Publishing who gave the go-ahead for this book. I would also like to thank CJ Rhoads for picking over my ramblings with a fine-tooth comb in editing this book. Len D'Innocenzo and Jack Cullen helped me get IPG started in the sales training business in 1994, and without their support and guidance I would not have been as successful.

My wife, Puja, has been encouraging me to write a book in the right way, with research, drafts, and more. I found this opportunity because my prior efforts were slipshod and she was honest and caring enough to tell me so. She also gave me the room, support, love, and time I needed to write.

My customers have given me a chance to learn and grow as I teach their people. Thanks to all of you who have had the confidence in my company and our ability to help you.

My brothers, Jack and Andy, and Debbie are always there for me, and always have been, which gives me support and strength, even at my weakest moments.

My children, Erica and Lizzy, although not having a direct impact on this book, have always encouraged me to write a book and provide me with the opportunity to love and be loved, which helps and sustains me.

Finally, to my parents who brought me onto this Earth and raised me in such a way that I have a strong survivor's instinct and the ability to read situations and people, which are my greatest sales assets.

Introduction

According to the *American Heritage Dictionary*, an *entrepreneur* is "a person who organizes, operates, and assumes the risk for a business venture." So in a sense, anyone who takes a risk on how much he or she earns, whose income is not guaranteed, is an entrepreneur. This could be a brand-new business owner, someone who invented and wants to sell something, a franchisor and its franchisees (selling the franchise to franchisees and then selling to end users), or a salesperson who gets paid a commission for what is sold in his or her territory or assignment. In all instances, perhaps more so at the beginning of your venture when you have no installed base of accounts, the role of effective sales is critical to your success.

This book discusses the critical elements of selling, from targeting and prospecting to closing and negotiating. It is relevant for anyone who is selling anything. It will give you multiple ideas you can easily implement, most at a very low investment cost. The biggest investment you will have to make is your time and effort, without which any entrepreneurial or sales effort will fail.

Many people believe that selling is different based on different products or services. This is almost entirely a false premise. True, you need to know your product; the idiosyncrasies, language, or acronyms an industry uses; competitive offerings and differences; and so forth. It's also true that certain aspects or skills of selling might be more pronounced based on what you are selling. However, the basic elements of selling are the same, regardless of product, service, industry, and even country.

Too many salespeople and companies rely on their products to sell themselves. They are too reliant on the advantages or popularity of a product. They expect that prospects will be so excited, and see the advantages so clearly, that they will buy just by seeing the product. When the product is new, popularity and uniqueness often carry the sale. Apple's iPod or the iPhone, when they were first released, are good examples of this (and are still, which is testimony to Apple's innovation and uniqueness). But what happens when the excitement and advantage are gone? Because the salespeople have developed the bad or sloppy sales habits of letting the product offerings convince the prospect to buy (versus selling the advantages of the product), they are now at a real deficit. They fail once their product or service loses some of its advantage.

Don't get me wrong; it is always great to have a significant product or service advantage, but you should always sell as if you don't. As long as you have a competitive product with a large enough market, all you need to do is know how to sell well and you will be successful.

In 1994, I founded the Improved Performance Group (IPG), which focuses on sales, pre- and post-sales customer support, and management training. I have an excellent product, but there are thousands of sales training companies that feel the same way. At the time of this writing, I Googled "sales training," and 26,200,000 hits came up. Many of my competitors are much bigger. They spend much more money marketing their services. They pay high fees so they land on the first page when Googled. So why do people and companies buy my company's services? Because I *know how to sell* and can teach others how to sell in both good and bad economies.

The year 2001 was a horrible business year for three reasons. The first: The Y2K craze was over (the year 2000 was the impending event of the millennium; everyone had to do something to make sure the programs on their computer systems worked properly). Second, the Internet boom busted and Wall Street was a shambles. Third was the horror of 9/11. I was in a panic, but I analyzed what industries were still doing well (or might even do better) and where my services were best suited. I didn't do as well as in the boom years preceding, but I was very happy with my company's performance. The year 2008 was also bad economically, but—based on the same approach this book outlines—sales went extremely well. This year (2009) looks even worse, but my approach will help offset the economic downturn.

Unlike most sales books that address a piece, stage, or "moment" of the sales process, this book will address selling as a holistic process, delineating how each part of the sales process positively or negatively affects each other (see Table I.1 and Table 2.1). This knowledge will significantly increase your ability to sell more. Examples include:

- Starting a sales opportunity in your "Sweet Spot," so you are ahead of the competition from the beginning.
- Creating an environment in which people feel more comfortable with you so they tell you more and listen more to what you say.
- Having a full "sales funnel" and its impact on your ability to sell and negotiate more effectively.
- Employing "Benefits[3]"—showing benefits from three perspectives: technical, business/financial, and individual/company—which is the most powerful way of presenting or proposing your offer.
- Brainstorming solutions so you can differentiate your offer as much as possible.
- Prospecting in the twenty-first century using the Internet, Web 2.0 applications, and other technologies to reach more people.

- Having a competitive product and being the best salesperson (as opposed to relying on having the best product to sell).
- Presenting over the phone, web, or in person.
- Customizing your presentations and demonstrations to increase your percentage of wins.
- Eliminating or softening objections to accelerate sales cycles and make your negotiations easier.
- Handling the most common negotiation issues or tactics.
- Maintaining the highest level of confidence so you sell more.
- Avoiding the emotional roller coaster of selling, including dealing with stress and rejection.

I'll provide stories to illustrate key points, tools, and forms you can use to increase sales, and R.E.A.L. (Relevant, Effective, Applied Learning) Tips and Reminders for your use.

I believe that if you master the elements described in this book, you will be in the top echelon of salespeople and your business will thrive. E-mail me if you have any questions at JLondon@ipgtraining.com or visit my website at ipgtraining.com.

Good luck and good selling!

Table I.1
Skills Needed at Different Stages of the Sale. (Steps and terms to be explained as we proceed.)

Stage	Stage 1: Identify "Sweet Spot"	Stage 2: Prospect	Stage 3: Qualify and Discover	Stage 4: Present, Propose or Demonstrate (PPD)	Stage 5: Negotiate and Close
Purpose	Research territory based on "Sweet Spot"	Prospect and get first meeting	Establish mutual interest and understand priorities, needs, and personal gain. Begin to qualify, fit to your Sweet Spot, and see how serious prospect is about buying	PPD your solution with TTV/ROI	Negotiate, agree on pricing, terms and close deal
Key Elements	• Research territory • Research companies • Create target account list	• Prepare call • Use Internet, Web 2.0, and references to find legitimate reasons to call • Call people who would benefit from your solution	• Develop rapport, comfort, and credibility • Understand current situation and environment, priorities, needs, and personal gain • Identify compelling event	• Present, demonstrate, or provide proposal • Align with S.PRI.N.G. Dialogue, DiSC • Set traps for competition	• Prepare for negotiation try. To have all parties on both sides in attendance • Agree on Ts and Cs business conditions, and pricing • Get signature on contract or commitment on date to do so

• Enter into sales database	• Get commitment to meet • Confirm meeting over phone or internet • Pick up and adapt for DiSC[a] style	• Understand procurement process • Identify key contacts • Identify competition • Identify criteria • Assess propensity to buy, incl. budget, financial condition, culture, procurement history • Plant seeds to see if there is a fit; influence thinking; and set traps for competition	• Close for next step

(Continued)

Table I.1 (*Continued*)
Skills Needed at Different Stages of the Sale. (Steps and terms to be explained as we proceed.)

Key Elements			Establish next step/s		
Skills	• Territory Mgmt. • Resource Mgmt.	• Prospect and Gain Access to Power • S.PRI.N.G. Dialogue • DiSC • Objection Handling • Close to Next Step	• Team Selling • S.PRI.N.G. Dialogue • DiSC • Listening • Close to Next Step	• Presenting • DiSC • Objection Handling • Listening • Close to Next Step	• Negotiations • Objection Handling • DiSC • Team Selling • Objection Handling • Close for Order

[a]DiSC refers to Dominant, Influential, Steady, Conscientious. Discussed in more detail in Chapter 3.

1

Nobody Wants What You Are Selling

Nobody wants what you are selling! It seems paradoxical to say that in a book about selling. The truth is people only want what you are selling if: (1) You can help them get what they want or (2) Help them avoid what they don't want on a technical (product), professional/financial (business, career, money), and/or personal level (personal being the most important). And the sooner the better!

EMBRACE THE PERSPECTIVE

If you embrace this perspective, it will change the way you sell and place you in the upper echelons of salespeople. It changes your perspective because you will spend more time understanding a prospect's professional and business priorities rather than talking about your product or service. This will give you more information for when you do present your product or service.

True Story 1

Mary, a salesperson I was observing, was meeting with Sharon, a Director of IT (Information Technologies). Sharon's company had just merged with another. Prior to this merger, Mary had been working on a proposal to have Sharon renew a contract that was expiring.

Mary went into the meeting and after exchanging pleasantries began to talk about the proposal as if nothing had changed. Sharon's answers were very short and curt, which surprised Mary because she thought they had a good relationship. I couldn't let this go on so I asked Sharon if we could step back and discuss the merger, her thoughts, concerns, how this affected her and the people who worked for her, etc. Her manner changed entirely, and she began to express her concerns, confusion, and more. Incorporating Sharon's perspective helped us to get to the details we needed to write the proposal that helped Sharon address her technical, professional, and (most important) personal concerns and priorities—which were mostly about keeping her job.

True Story 2

In 1976 I was buying my first new car since getting married. I did most of the research and had narrowed it down to a Volkswagen (VW) or Honda Civic. I was torn because both had qualities I really liked. I kept going back and forth to each dealer asking questions. I was at the VW dealer for the umpteenth time, and the salesperson said, "You have been here many times and I have never really asked you about yourself. Are you married?" "Yes, I am," I replied. "Do you have kids?" "Yes, we just had a little girl, Erica. She is three months old." "Well," he said, "let me show you all the tremendous safety features of the car you are looking at." And he proceeded to do so.

I never went back to the Honda dealer. Why? Because the VW salesperson related and presented the car to me at a level that was much more important than miles per gallon—or zero to sixty speed ratings. He talked about how safe it would be for Erica and my wife. I already was comfortable with the technical and financial aspects. He sold me on the more personal aspects (in retrospect, if he had asked me earlier, he may have shortened the sales cycle significantly because the Honda didn't have any of the safety features he showed me).

Think about any recent purchase you have made. Think about the reasons you chose the product or service that you chose, no matter how significant or insignificant. You will see that all kinds of personal biases and preferences filter and influence your decisions. When you are selling, discover what biases and preferences influence the person to whom you are trying to sell and you will sell more.

What do people want when they buy something? Some possibilities:

more money	to see their kids more
more recognition	to save money
safety and stability	to provide for their family
time	to have a competitive advantage
fewer problems	to get promoted
less chaos	more attention
greater success	to work more easily

Why did you buy this book? What do you want this book to do for you? Get a piece of paper and pencil and answer these questions:

- What do you want professionally and personally?
- What does it mean if you get these things (desire)?
- What if you don't get them or lose what you already have (fear)?

The answers to these questions are extremely insightful—they explain most of what you do and why.

Now let's figure out the underlying motives of your prospects and customers for the product or service you are selling. In general, what do your customers or prospects want from your offerings? Enter your information on the same piece of paper you just used.

- What do they want professionally and personally?
- What does it mean if they get these things (desire)?
- What if they don't get them or lose them (fear)?

I hope you can you see how powerful the items are that you wrote down. These are the reasons that people take action and make decisions. If your customers can't see how your offering addresses their fears and desires, they won't buy it. Or, if someone else does a better job in addressing their fears and desires, they will buy from them rather than you.

SELLING TO PEOPLE'S DiSC® PROFILE AND PREFERENCES

The DiSC®* profile (now offered by Inscape Publishing) has been around since the early 1960s with more than thirty-seven million people worldwide using the profile to get insight into their behavior. It is based on Dr. William Marston's studies of "the emotions of normal people" done in the 1920s. Marston's studies and findings also influenced the invention of the polygraph machine. In summary, his studies showed that human behavior is

- observable
- situationally based
- flexible
- dynamic

DiSC categorizes human behavior into four primary areas or behavior styles. We have all four of these, but one or two tend to be more pronounced than others depending upon the situation, and can change if the situation is different. For example, you might behave differently at work than you do at home, or when you are in a foreign country for the first time versus someplace you have been many times.

What is critical to understand is even though you may behave differently in different situations, you will behave the same in similar situations. So when you are selling, you will behave the same way. Prospects, when they are buying, will behave, or buy, the same way. Each style has its own preferences as seen in Table 1.1.

As salespeople, we should be aware that these behavioral traits are one of the factors that drive people to take action. We can help people get what they want, and avoid what they don't want, on many levels, including—and sometimes most importantly—from a behavioral perspective. DiSC will be discussed more fully in Chapter 3.

---

*DiSC® by Inscape Publishing, Inc. All rights reserved. Used by permission of Inscape Publishing, Inc.

Table 1.1
DiSC® Desires and Fears

DiSC® Style	Desire	Fear
Dominant	Control, power, and results	Being out of control, taken advantage of, and failure
Influential	Influence, results, and being liked or popular	Not being liked or paid attention to
Steadfast	Stability, cooperation, maintenance of status quo	Change, conflict, instability
Conscientious	Perfection, quality, and accuracy	Being criticized for poor quality or making a mistake

R.E.A.L. TIPS AND REMINDERS

R.E.A.L. stands for *R*elevant, *E*ffective, *A*pplied *L*earning.

- ☑ Remember that you are not selling a product or service. You are helping people get what they want (desire) or avoid what they don't want (fear).
- ☑ Be aware of people's pace and tone of voice. It will immediately tell you to adjust what you are experiencing and make the person you are selling to more comfortable with you.
- ☑ Desire and fear are very strong motivators for a prospect to take action. Don't be afraid to seek to understand and ask what would happen if a person or project failed.
- ☑ People want things on many levels, the personal being the most important. The more immediate the impact you have on helping people, the more likely they will buy.

2

The Art of Selling

Selling is a holistic process in which multiple things are happening at once (i.e. adjusting to people's DiSC style, anticipating objections, listening, preparing your next question, presenting your solution, etc.), and each step and event in a sales process positively or negatively affects what happens next.

ONE THING LEADS (OR DOESN'T LEAD) TO ANOTHER

Many of the variables involved in a sale or sales process are within your control. These include:

- How many good opportunities you are working simultaneously (also known as your sales pipeline or funnel), which will give you more or less confidence throughout the selling cycle.
- How good or poor a fit your product or service is to the prospect's priorities and needs, and if you should even be trying to sell it in the first place.
- How well you get along with the person you are selling to; at one end of the spectrum, they love you, and at the other, they wouldn't buy from you if you paid them to.
- How much time have you spent with the person/s you are trying to sell versus the competition, who might have a better relationship.
- How well have you positioned your product or service versus the competition's offerings.
- Whether you have the information you need about their buying process (people involved in the decision influencing the buyer) and their criteria, or whether you are selling into a vacuum.
- Whether you know how much money they have to spend.
- Your mood at the time you are speaking to the prospect and whether you are distracted or focused.
- How well you have set traps for the competition.
- Whether you are talking to the right person/people who can make or influence a decision.

- How well or poorly you have differentiated yourself.
- To what extent you know if the buyer is really interested (is there are a compelling or impending event?) or just "kicking tires."

Handling these items well, together, can dramatically improve your results. They are the ingredients in the art of selling. But keep in mind also that there are a number of variables that are not in your control:

- The economy. Is it thriving to the point people are more willing to spend money? Is it in a lull or recession where people are very reluctant to spend?
- Competitive products.
- The prospects' mood when you meet with them and other variables that are affecting their propensity to buy.
- How well or poorly your prospects, or their businesses, are doing.
- Other things that are legitimately more important to them than buying what you are selling.
- Something personal going on in their life.
- Internal politics of a decision.
- They have a friend or relative working for your competitor (this happened to me twice in the last six months).

WHAT CAN YOU DO?

Several of these variables can work for or against you. Let's take a look at a few of the more important ones in detail. In each case, you'll want to work to stand on the "for you" side of the issue.

How Full or Empty Is Your Sales Funnel?

For You: When you have a lot of opportunities, you are more confident, you don't panic, and you don't discount unnecessarily. You also tend not to "chase" or "pursue" bad business. Life is good!

Against You: The opposite of everything above. You don't have a lot of opportunities. You are nervous, insecure, or indifferent because you feel defeated and believe nobody wants to buy from you. You waste time trying to sell in situations where the odds are against you and your close rates are poor, which adds to your sense of defeat and lack of confidence. Everything suffers, personally and professionally.

How Good or Poor a Fit Is Your Product or Service for the Prospect's Priorities and Needs?

For You: You should only sell to opportunities where there is a good or great fit. Doing anything else is self-defeating. Likewise, your prospect will know if there is a fit. It is like trying on a piece of clothing or a glove. If it fits, you know it, and it makes you feel good and you are more open to buying it than if it doesn't. Your job is to get their measurements first so you can see as quickly as possible if there is a fit or not.

Against You: Trying to sell something that isn't a good fit is like trying to draw into a straight when you play poker and all you have is two of the five cards you need. The odds are extremely low, so it is better to fold as early as possible and not lose your money. Or to continue from the example above, trying to fit the customer into size thirty-four pants when he has a size forty waist.

How Well Do You Know Your Offering/Product?

Do you know your product very well? How well can you position it?

For You: If you know your offering really well, you will be able to pick, choose, and present the elements of it that are most relevant to the prospect and different from the competition. It has an intensity like a laser cutting through a hard substance.

Against You: If you don't know your offering, everything will be general, you will pick or choose too many elements that are unrelated, and your offering will appear bland to the prospect—like a dim twenty-five-watt lightbulb.

Do You Get Along with the Prospect?

Do you get along with the people to whom you are selling?

For You: If you do, then the people will naturally be more open to you, which will result in them telling you more and being more open to what you say.

Against You: If you don't get along, the people will not want to buy from you if they have another choice. Even if they want your product, if they can buy it from someone else, they will.

Let's stop at this point and look at the cumulative effect of these three elements. If you have a lot of opportunities in the funnel AND your offering is a good or great fit to the prospect's priorities AND you get along well with the prospect, then your selling environment is very positive and you are in a good position.

Conversely, if you do not have a lot in the funnel AND your offering is poorly positioned in relation to the strengths of your fit AND you don't get along well with the prospect, then your selling environment is very negative and it is doubtful you will make a sale.

Let's continue ...

How Much Time Have You Spent?

Have you spent enough time with the people to whom you are trying to sell? (This is particularly important when your offering is similar to the competition's, because it could be the deciding factor.)

> *For You:* The more time you spend with someone during a sales process and get along with them, a relationship begins to build where the person to whom you are selling feels a little bit more of a commitment and obligation to you. For example, if prospects spend time and money traveling to see you, discuss their issues, discuss plans, review materials sent, etc., the more likely they are to trust you and want to buy from you.
>
> *Against You:* If the prospect only gets a brochure about your offer, and has not spent much time reviewing it, she has committed less time and money and is less likely to buy. A prospect is more willing to move things back or postpone if she hasn't given much attention to the buying process.

Do You Have the Information You Need?

The information you need includes their priorities, needs, and criteria. Are you selling into a vacuum, without the information you need?

> *For You:* When you know a person's or company's priorities and criteria, you are much better able to position, present, or demonstrate your offering. You can be more specific about your offering and its relevance to the buyer's situation.
>
> *Against You:* Without this knowledge, you are selling into a vacuum. You are guessing, and because of that, you might present everything, diluting the most essential elements of your offering. In addition, your presentations will tend to be too long and lose the attention of people to whom you are presenting.

Are You Talking to the Right Person?

Are you talking to the right person or the right group of people? Can they make the decision?

> *For You:* "The right people" means they are the decision makers or they influence the decision maker. Further, they are probably tied to the money that needs to be spent. They are the people who are having the problem that needs to be addressed or goal to be achieved. Finally, they usually have the authority and DiSC style to do something about the problem.
>
> *Against You:* You could have the best relationship and make the best presentation or demonstration of your offering, but if it is to someone who has none of the attributes described above, you are wasting your time. Pack up your bags and find someone better qualified. These people are hopers, time wasters, tire kickers. The only time you should ever spend time with these people is if you are selling something where

a lot of education needs to be done up front or it is a brand-new category that people have never seen. (We will cover this in more detail in the section on Gaining Access to Power and S.PRI.N.G. Dialogue).

How Well Have You Differentiated Yourself?

Have you differentiated yourself well or poorly?

For You: During the sales cycle, you need to differentiate yourself and your offering from the competition's offering. You need to differentiate your approach from their approach. This can be done in many ways, including using terms and acronyms from the prospect's industry, demonstrating a greater knowledge of things relevant to the prospect, using your resources more effectively, presenting or proposing the aspects of your solution (hopefully unique) in relation to their priorities, needs, personal gain, and more. You can also differentiate yourself by how responsive you are, how prepared you are, how much knowledge and professionalism you display, and how well you get along with the prospect.

Against You: If you have not differentiated yourself, your product will be seen as a commodity with no added value, and people will either buy something else, beat you up for a lower price, or do nothing at all. If your product is seen as a commodity, price matters; prospects won't see why they should pay more for the same product or service.

Are They Really Interested?

Are they really interested? Is there a compelling or impending event? Or are they just "kicking tires," and probably won't end up buying anything at all, from anyone?

For You: This one is huge. People will not buy something unless there is something or someone driving them to do so. You can know this by asking and understanding what or who is driving their interest, and the sooner you know, the better. Is there a compelling event (something they should do) or imminent event (something they must do) that is driving their interest?

This is especially true when you are selling something that is new and unique. People will want to see it, even if they have no intention of buying it—and that might be necessary to create interest. However, do not mistake that for buying something immediately. It might become a sale, but in the future.

Against You: When I was part of a group first selling videoconferencing, it got everyone's attention. Everyone wanted to see a demonstration. It was like *The Jetsons'* cartoon world come true. The demos always went well because the product was so innovative and exciting. It was critical for us to understand "what" and "who" was behind their interest, or we would end up wasting our time, chasing business that was non-existent. We had to focus on real business opportunities by more deeply qualifying their interest.

SELLING WELL TAKES PREPARATION

You can see how all these elements affect one another. You make a great presentation but to the wrong person. You prospect often but to the wrong demographic or fit. You are an expert in your product but do nothing to adjust your style so people are comfortable with you. You rely on your offering to do all of your selling so you don't bother to understand the specific requirements of a sale and your offering loses much of its luster. The variables are innumerable that make selling such an exciting and thrilling profession.

Think about selling as a hundred-meter race to the finish line of closing a deal. If you start off in the right place, in your "Sweet Spot" (discussed in detail in Chapter 4), you already have a twenty-meter head start due to your fit, references, or experiences. If you are talking to the right people and get along with them to create a comfortable selling environment, you are increasing your lead. And finally, if you understand their requirements, processes, and criteria so well that your presentation is exact and impactful, you are in a wonderful position to close the deal and win the race. It doesn't mean you will win 100 percent of the time, but you will have a higher closing ratio.

Another way to look at how the variables work for you or against you is to place them into the steps of a sales cycle, as shown in Table 2.1. We will be going over these steps in the chapters to come.

Table 2.1
Sales Cycle Steps

Steps in Sales Cycle	For You	Against You
Prospecting or Attracting Prospects	You know your target market and are focusing your efforts and money properly.	You don't know and you are trying to attract anyone with a pulse. You waste money and time. You market and prospect to a general audience vs. a specific target best suited for your offer. It would be like spending money and taking time selling "ice to the Eskimos."
Qualifying and Discovery	You do an excellent job of understanding what they want and how you can help them. You have also found a way to make the prospect comfortable with you so they are more trusting, open up to you, tell you more, and listen to what you have to say.	You have started in the wrong place, so you are already in a bad place. You are feeling pressured so you don't take the time to understand the prospect's requirements, and since you are feeling pressured, your sensitivity to them is poor and you develop no rapport or trust at all.

Presenting, Proposing, or Demonstrating Your Solution	Since you did such a great job building rapport and understanding their specific priorities, requirements, and needs, you can customize your proposal, presentation, or demonstration. They can see the relevance and positive effect it will have for them professionally and/or personally. They are also more receptive since you are presenting to their DiSC style.	You do little or no discovery and just talk about or present your solution. It has no direct relevance since you cannot verbalize or demonstrate how it works to the benefit of the person/s or company. It would be like presenting all of the incredible features of a brand-new video camera to someone who has never owned a camera and just wants to take pictures of simple, nonmoving objects. Since you never asked about their requirements in the previous steps, you throw everything at them hoping something sticks.
Handling Objections	There will definitely be fewer objections if you have done all the things described in the previous steps. This isn't to say there won't be any objections, but there will be fewer and their intensity will be diminished. Most importantly, they will be in the context of wanting to buy something from you vs. having no interest at all.	The objections and resistance will be many and intense. Since there is no rapport, nor does the prospect really see how it will help, they have nothing to lose by saying, "No, not interested," or really being aggressive about you dropping your price, which helps nobody if your product or service doesn't help them. You end up with an unhappy customer at a very low profit.
Negotiating and Closing	Pretty much the same as above. Negotiations are done in a more comfortable environment (this is not to say that people won't be acrimonious and tough), but they want what you are selling. You can respond to their issues and concerns more effectively and prevent excessive discounting or giving away of things since you can constantly relate the value and benefit of your offer.	Without rapport, time spent with the prospect, and positioning the relevance of your offer, people will be harsh negotiators and take a very hard stance. You will have little to persuade them with, either professionally or personally, and you will probably not win the sale. If you do, it will not be under the best of circumstances, nor will it yield additional business.

R.E.A.L. TIPS AND REMINDERS

- ☑ Start off on the right foot. Understand the best places to sell based upon your solution's unique offerings or where it has a strong track record. This is always important, even more so in a down economy.
- ☑ Prospect and market as much as possible to the people, industries, or departments in companies that have the best fit (much more on this in Chapter 4).
- ☑ Try (it is not easy) to get to the decision makers and the people who can most benefit from your offer.
- ☑ Be sensitive to people's DiSC style and their preferences when they buy things. Adapt your style to theirs so they are comfortable with you.
- ☑ Try to understand what their priorities, needs, gain, goals, and objectives are first before you talk too much about your product or service.
- ☑ When you do talk about your offering, try and relate it back as much as possible to what they have told you is important to them.
- ☑ Try to have them commit something to the sales process so they "buy in" and it is hard for them to delay, postpone, or go with someone else.
- ☑ Don't chase bad business. If you do a good job qualifying up front, you will know if there is a good fit and if you are talking to the right people at the right time (they have a need at the time you are speaking with them versus just information gathering).
- ☑ If you have enough in the funnel of good opportunities, you will be able to walk away from bad business more easily. This is not easy to do but easier if you have a lot of good prospects working.
- ☑ Take time to adjust your "standard" presentations so they relate as much as possible to the sales opportunity.

3

People Buy from People

The expression "people buy from people" has been around since I started selling in 1975, so I imagine it has been around far longer than that. It means that if a prospect likes, trusts, finds you comfortable to be with, and feels you are competent and honest, they will be more likely to buy from you. Unless you are selling entirely without human interaction (Internet, mail order, etc.) or the prospect has no other option, a good relationship is a critical element of being a great salesperson.

CREATING THE ENVIRONMENT

How does a salesperson create this kind of environment? Staying with the idea that one thing always affects another in selling, the process actually starts in choosing the demographics, departments, or applications that your offering is best suited for. Let's say you are selling a low-end digital camera. You would probably sell this to first-time buyers, or people with a certain budget in mind. If you decided to sell that to someone who is looking for the latest, high-end camera, he probably wouldn't be very interested, or find you credible and trustworthy, because you would be trying to sell them something they outgrew many years ago. The same is true if you tried to sell the most expensive, advanced, feature-rich camera to a six-year-old.

Another popular saying is that people buy in the following order (although they are probably not conscious of this):

- You
- Your company
- Your solution

This is particularly true if you are selling something that is not very well known, doesn't have a big company name behind it, and is a leading-edge product. (Incidentally, this has been my sales experience my entire career.)

Let's break down each element:

Element	Variables
You	Pacing, commonality, knowledge, experience, listening, empathy, responsiveness, honesty, relatedness
Company	Background, stability, support, finances, history, references
Solution	Fit to prospect's needs, time on market, stability, support, cost, references

Pacing

Have you ever been with someone you like or care about who moves faster or slower than you? If you have, you know how frustrating it can be. Have you ever been with someone who offers too much or little information? Again: very frustrating. Have you ever been in a situation where both are occurring at the same time? Maddening, to the point where you might not even want to be with the person.

Now imagine the same scenario when you are trying to sell to someone. They don't know you, have no obligation to you, and they are experiencing what was just described above. Your chances of selling that person are slim and none (and slim just walked out the door). Later in this chapter we discuss a way of avoiding this using the DiSC model.

Other ways of pacing (or "mirroring," as it is often called) are physical, which is quite often done on an unconscious level. For example, if your arms are crossed, your prospects might also cross their arms (or vice versa). Or if one is leaning back in a chair or speaking in a certain way, the other might as well. Doing this on a conscious level, being aware of it (without being obvious about it) is another way of making people feel more comfortable with you.

How do we do this more effectively? Again we need to go back to the idea of what happens before you even meet someone. Are you prepared and relaxed enough to pick up and mirror the signals the person is giving you, or are you too wound up to do so? Do you go in with a receptive, open, empathetic listening manner—or a telling, forceful, fixed, unreceptive manner? If you do the latter, you will be less able to respond to the subtle messages and signals people send you, and therefore not adapt or mirror them so they are comfortable with you.

The DiSC Profile

As mentioned in Chapter 1, one of the first known references to the study of human behavior goes back to the days of the Greeks, almost five thousand years ago, and nothing much has changed except most people don't wear togas anymore (except during the Halloween Parade in New York City). Each style has its own characteristics and preferences, as can be seen in Table 3.1.

As salespeople, we need to be aware that desire and fear are important factors that drive people to take action. Conversely, if they don't, people will do nothing. Selling is helping people get what they want and avoiding what they don't want on many levels, including and maybe most importantly, from a personal or behavioral perspective.

The most effective way to know which DiSC style your prospects might be is to pick up on their pace (fast or slow), tone (friendly or serious), and how much data they want (a lot or little). Then mirror that subtly by tapping into your own behavior style that matches the prospects'. Table 3.2 lays this out for you.

Another way to think about DiSC is as if it were a language with the three main elements being pace, tone, and information. Just as with any language, it is easy to recognize the language but hard to speak it unless you study and apply it. For example, if you were walking down a street, you could probably identify someone speaking French or Spanish or German, but you probably couldn't speak it back unless you had studied it. Being able to identify a language is useless unless you can speak it back. Speaking DiSC means adjusting your pace, tone, and information to the person you are speaking with. It sounds simple, but it takes practice.

True Story

It was the second year of my company, the Improved Performance Group. A friend of mine who worked at a very large manufacturer of

Table 3.1
DiSC® Style and Characteristics

DiSC® Style	Pace	Tone of Voice	Desire	Fear
Dominant	Fast	Dominant, assertive, confident, impatient	Control, power, and results	Being out of control, taken advantage of, and failure
Influential	Fast	Expressive, outgoing, wordy	Influence, results, and being liked or popular	Not being liked
Steadfast	Slower	Calm, easy, comfortable, supportive	Stability, cooperation, maintenance of status quo	Change, conflict
Conscientious	Slower	Analytical, removed, cynical	Perfection, quality, and accuracy	Being criticized for poor quality

Table 3.2
Matching a Prospect's DiSC® Style

DiSC® Style	Pace	Tone of Voice	Amount of Information
Dominant	Fast	Dominant, assertive, confident, impatient	Less, use bullet points, be direct and to the point, focus on control and results
Influential	Fast	Expressive, outgoing, wordy	More than the D but not so much as the S or C, be more positive and effusive, paint a big picture
Steadfast	Slower	Calm, easy, comfortable, supportive	Lots, with a focus on how things are done, processes, stability
Conscientious	Slower	Analytical, removed, cynical	The most of all styles, with a focus on perfection, quality, and accuracy—the more independent and unbiased, the better

personal computers told me they were evaluating vendors to train their salespeople. He introduced me to the person in charge, and we set up a meeting to introduce me and my company's capabilities in person. However, because I was late to the process, he was only willing to give me thirty minutes with him and his team. I was pumped. This was the opportunity I needed. Business was good and I was busy, but nothing as large as this. I prepared (while I was doing everything else an entrepreneur does) and flew from New York City to their headquarters in Texas. I was very excited. Unfortunately, I was also very tired and overcaffeinated.

The meeting got off to a bad start because more people attended than I had prepared materials for. (Lesson learned: Always bring more material than expected.) He had somebody go copy some of the materials but wanted to start while they were doing so because we had limited time. In my normal, High D(ominant) NYC manner, I told him I would rather wait. To me, my request and tone were fine. To him, it filled every stereotype of a New Yorker. Because I only had thirty minutes, once I got started I made a fatal error in talking, talking, talking versus spending some time getting to know them and taking a more relaxed approach (we were in the South and it was a big company so it was a bit more slower paced and laid back).

Long story short, after the meeting the gentleman took me aside and said, "Thanks for coming down. That style may work in New York, but it doesn't down here in Texas." I didn't win that deal. In retrospect, even if I had been perfect I probably wouldn't have won the deal. They saw me as a way to provide a courtesy to my friend but were too far down the process to let anyone else in. (Another lesson—try to be first to influence criteria and relations, and know the decision-making process.) One ironic note: the company's sales force had a saying, "Moving at the Speed of Light," which related to how fast things moved in their sales environment, but this gentleman and his committee made the decision in "High S" fashion. The result of their decision was that the company invested millions of dollars in a program that was a complete failure. Why? In part because they chose a program that fit their comfort level as High S's that was big, well-known, and safe. Unfortunately for them, the expensive program did not take into consideration the style of people who would be using it—who were very "High D" and "i" (influencers).

Fortunately for me, I had another chance a few years later. This time I won the deal because I was involved in the decision-making process earlier, had learned from my previous errors, and modified my style so the buyer was much more comfortable with me. They were one of my best customers for four years, and I trained more than a thousand of their people.

Think of a situation, past or future. What could you have done (or can you do now) to be more aware of your prospect's DiSC style?

Building Comfort, Trust, and Credibility

People will buy from people they "like" and trust. As a salesperson, there are many things we can do throughout a sales process to do this and differentiate ourselves from others. This is crucial. If people have a choice, they will inevitably choose someone they are more comfortable with.

"You" consists of many elements:

Compatibility	Sincerity
Commonality	Pacing
Competency	Experience
Language	Listening
Knowledge	Empathy
Honesty	Background
Follow-through	Professionalism

Let's break down some of these elements.

Compatibility: DiSC, beliefs, attitude, "chemistry."

Commonality: Background, common business or personal experiences, likes/dislikes, where you grew up, where you shop, hobbies, sports.

Competency: Competency is preparation, knowledge, experience, and follow-up.

Language: Of course the language of the person you are speaking with, but even better the language of her business or the environment you are discussing, especially using acronyms.

Knowledge: Knowledge about your product, the industry, or environment the prospective customers are in. This also means knowledge about the prospect specifically and the business environment generally.

Honesty: Do you say "no" to things you can't do or don't know about? Do you "spin" everything so you fall into the stereotype of a bad salesperson? Do you say "no" to business that isn't good for you? Do you admit vulnerabilities or show emotions?

Follow-through: Follow-through is apparent from your very first interaction. Do you send a thank-you and confirm your next steps? Do you get people the information you promised in the time frame you committed, or even earlier? Do you set the right expectations so people know when things will happen (Hint for "High i's": give yourself more time because you tend to be the least organized and love to talk).

Empathy: American Heritage Dictionary defines *empathy* as "Identification with and understanding of another's situation, feelings, and motives. The attribution of one's own feelings to an object." Are you putting yourself in their shoes? Can you hear what they are saying and feeling, even if they don't tell you? Are you truly concerned and want to help them or really only want to sell them something? Can you imagine the minutia of what they are telling you about? Can you feel their feelings (excitement, worry, concern, happiness, etc.)? Do you know your product or service well enough that you relate back to them how your product or service will help them or are your offerings too generic? People can feel what you are feeling about them. And they will respond accordingly.

Sincerity: Dictionary.com defines *sincere* as "free of deceit, hypocrisy, or falseness; earnest." Are you sincere about wanting to sell somebody something that he will be happy with? Are you sincere about your belief and confidence in the product or service you are selling? Are you honest? Are you grounded enough in yourself to make the sincerity shine through?

Listening: Perhaps the most important skill is to be a good listener. According to Inscape Publishing (the same company that offers the DiSC Profiles) there are five primary ways to listen, each appropriate in different situations:

- *Appreciative:* Listens in a relaxed manner, seeking enjoyment, entertainment, or inspiration.
- *Empathic:* Listens without judging, is supportive of the speaker, and learns from the experiences of others. If people feel that you heard their internal struggles, and have the sense that you got it, they will be more open to you.
- *Comprehensive:* Listens to organize and make sense of information by understanding relationships among ideas.
- *Discerning:* Listens to get complete information, understands the main message, and determines important details.
- *Evaluative:* Listens to make a decision based on information provided and may accept or reject message based on personal beliefs.

My experience in teaching salespeople shows that most people are very good at all the listening styles except empathic, which is ironic because empathic listening is often noted as the most important by these same people.

A very powerful way for you to experience the power of empathic listening is to think of a time in your life when you truly felt heard, where the person you were talking to had no objective or motive except to be there for you (a friend, doctor, mentor, parent, etc.). What did it feel like and how do you think listening like this would help you as a salesperson?

How do you become an empathic listener? Try to remove anything that might distract you when speaking to someone (other things to do, people interrupting you, things you are worried about, another meeting, etc.). Listen not only for the words but also for the underlying issues (desires, fears, and concerns). The more people feel you get what they are saying, the more they will trust you and feel safer with you. Put these into words for the person as a way of acknowledging them (sometimes known as "mirroring"). Also, the less pressured you feel (by being prepared, having a full funnel, etc.), the better you can hear what they are saying and feeling.

To foster empathy, come from a less cognitive space and a more emotional space. Let go of your own desires and fears while you are hearing them. Open up the process by making suggestions or summarizing what you have heard to create some momentum for them to talk. For example, "I hear you are saying this and I can also imagine that this is happening as well." Or, "I imagine that is scary." Or, "Sounds upsetting."

Don't be in a rush to talk. The more you hear, the more completely you can respond.

R.E.A.L. TIPS AND REMINDERS

☑ Put yourself in an environment where you won't be distracted. Sit with your back to a window or where your eyes might look away from the person you are speaking with.

☑ If on the phone, do the same thing. Close your door, or put up a sign letting people know you are on an important call.

☑ If in an open environment and on the phone, use headphones that cover both of your ears and cancel noise so you and your prospect won't be distracted.

☑ Don't rush into or out of a meeting. Space your appointments so you can stay focused while in them.

☑ Do things that others don't. Send a reminder before your appointment. Send a thank-you after an appointment. Send materials on a timely basis.

☑ Research your prospects and their industries as much as possible so you can relate to them as best as possible. Use some acronyms (properly, of course) from their industry to show competence.

☑ Before you meet, see if you have sold someone (person or company) with similar requirements so you can share the name (unless you are under a confidentiality agreement). Sharing the names of people who have purchased the same service or product makes people comfortable because they know they won't be the first person you have ever sold a product or service.

☑ Be prepared so you feel confident with your actions by doing some research about the person, and/or the company and/or the industry.

☑ Practice or prepare what you are going to ask or say. No matter how experienced you are, you will do better if you practice beforehand.

☑ Focus your efforts where you have the highest probability of success, where you naturally provide the most help.

☑ Dress appropriately. Not over- or underdressed. For example, if you were selling to a lawyer or bank, you would probably wear something more "professional." If you were selling to Web 2.0 consultants, a much more casual look would be appropriate.

☑ BE ON TIME! In fact be a little early. Nothing is worse than being late.

☑ If selling to a business, don't ask them what they do. Do a little research beforehand and mention a few things that they can comment on.

☑ Be sensitive to DiSC styles. Modify your pace, tone, and amount of information as soon as possible to make the other person comfortable with you.

☑ BE AN EXPERT in your field, and if possible, in theirs.

☑ Know your product or offering. People want to buy from people they trust, and knowledge of what you are selling is big.

☑ Be yourself. Whatever people find appealing about you outside of work they will find appealing about you in work.

4

Defining Your Sweet Spot

One of the most important elements of sales success is to try and sell your product or service as much as possible where you have a unique advantage, or the strongest fit possible. This is your "Sweet Spot." It is where you will win more often.

ATTACKING THE SWEET SPOT WITH A VENGEANCE

Once you've identified your Sweet Spot, you want to attack it with a vengeance.

True Story

My first job was selling Olivetti typewriters. At the time, I was twenty-two years old and clueless. My biggest competitor was IBM, which had approximately 93 percent market share. People would buy hundreds of IBM typewriters at list price and store them because they never knew when they would need one, and they were afraid they might not be able to get one from IBM in a timely fashion. It was a measure of prestige to have an IBM Selectric (see Figure 4.1) on your desk. More than once, I saw people hug their typewriter when I suggested they replace their IBM with an Olivetti. (I had to remind them that they were hugging a typewriter.)

In this environment, how was I supposed to succeed? After panicking for about ninety days, I asked for advice from a more experienced and successful salesperson who helped me see things with a clearer head. He suggested that I look at what my typewriter could do that IBM's couldn't. He also suggested that I concentrate on industries and applications where these unique capabilities might be critical to their business. That would give me an advantage over the almighty and powerful IBM.

So that's what I did. I made sure there was enough volume in these industries and applications to be successful, and that is all I focused on. I became much more intelligent about how and what people needed in these industries or applications. I learned the terms and acronyms they used so I

Figure 4.1
An IBM Selectric Typewriter

Photo courtesy of CJ Rhoads.

was much more credible. I was able to demonstrate and differentiate my product better. I could provide referrals in their industry that also made prospects more comfortable about buying a typewriter from the youthful me. I felt good about helping people in something that was a major part of their life. I didn't worry about other prospects that I might be missing. I knew I would get much better results with this kind of focus. By focusing, I became the number-one salesperson four years in a row. Since then, I have applied this concept to every sales or management position I have had, with the same exceptional results.

DEFINING YOUR "SWEET SPOT"

As entrepreneurs, we should be focusing on producing something different, better, and/or unique. We should be focusing on something better than what already exists in the market. As salespeople, we need to put our energy and effort into selling what is unique and different. It could be a brand-new product, service, or technology. Cars, personal computers, typewriters, and personal digital assistants (PDAs like the BlackBerry) were all, at one time, new products.

Or we could focus on a newer version of something that already exists. For example, we might sell a Honda automobile with better mileage, or a computer that is smaller, more powerful, and portable. Either way, there should be certain groups of people and companies that would be better suited for your offering than others. If there is not something unique, then you should know what you do extremely well or where your product is best suited. If neither of these exists, make sure your price is very low, find another occupation, or be an incredibly good salesperson.

The Story Continues

One of the most important reasons I was so successful at Olivetti is that I had knowledge about what my product did that my competition's product didn't (and the differences weren't many). To continue my story, the only differences between the Olivetti typewriter and the IBM Selectric were

1. The Olivetti could type on a horizontal, legal size piece of paper (fourteen-inches wide) whereas IBM could only type on an eleven-inch-wide (normal) piece of paper.
2. The Olivetti could do proportional spacing, the IBM could not.
3. The Olivetti could do architectural and engineering symbols, the IBM could not.

    If you are not old enough to remember, back then the way you changed your type style (also called a font) on a typewriter was by physically replacing the typing element (or ball) that was inside the typewriter. At the time, the typing element for the IBM had only fixed-spacing fonts—which means small letters (like an "i") took up the same amount of space as larger letters (like a "w").

    The Olivetti element could type with proportional spacing so that larger letters took up more space and smaller letters took up less space (just like a typeset printer), giving a much more professional look to typed documents. The Olivetti also had an element for architects and engineers with all types of symbols they use. (If at this point you are getting too excited about the amazing capabilities of the Olivetti, please take a few minutes to catch your breath and relax.)

That was it. Those were the only differences. How did this translate into success? I defined which industries and applications (departments in companies) required those differences: finance for the wide spreadsheets, legal for the quality proportional print, architectural and engineering groups for the architectural and engineering symbols.

Doing the Research

To figure out the specific strengths of your product or service and which industries might require those strengths, you can research it. Here's how:

- Start your venture utilizing previous experience and knowledge that helps you choose which product and service to offer.
- Investigate any previous experience the company, franchise, or division you belong to might have had with the product or service.
- Go to industry websites and review the useful information they may have.
- Attend trade shows (in person or virtual) and webinars to see what the competition is offering and what people are looking for.
- Do some secret shopping and see how competitors present their offerings.
- Call people who might give you insight.
- Go to the websites of companies that do a lot of research and offer it to the public. (For example, I have gotten lots of great stuff from IBM's website.)
- Review city or town websites. Quite often, a city or town will list the biggest companies and industries.
- Buy a mailing or e-mail list and do a survey to see what people want and need.
- Create a blog that asks people what they need, want, or is most important to them in choosing a product or service in your category.
- Just do a good old search on Google, Yahoo, Ask, etc., and see what pops up.

When I started my current company, IPG, I had previous knowledge and also called and wrote to people I knew to ask their opinion. I also reached out to companies and departments in the industries I thought were best to get their input. I tried not to get distracted by "what else" was out there. (Remember, everyone with salespeople needs sales training.) I needed to find my Sweet Spot to decide if there was enough business to be successful. Table 4.1 is an example from my Olivetti experience of how I categorized the information into a useable format.

To determine this information for your own products or services, begin to define the following:

- Is there anything about your products, services, or company that gives you an advantage or instances where you or others have been successful?
- Who (people, industries, or departments in a company) would benefit from this most?
- What activities or applications are in high volume in your territory that your company or service addresses better than others?

Use the Internet, industry websites, online databases, blogs, social networks, business networks, local magazines, Chambers of Commerce, Better Business Bureaus, etc. to research. Is there a specific industry that is predominant in your assignment, company, industry, city, state, or franchise? Does one stand out that should take more of your time and energy? Are you particularly knowledgeable in any area that you can leverage? You can use Table 4.2 to record your own findings.

Table 4.1
Matching Differentiators to Industries, an Example

Differentiators or Areas of Success	Person, Industry, Application That Needs This	Title of Person to Contact	Companies or Applications or Departments
Olivetti could type architectural engineering symbols	Architecture and engineering departments of universities	Dean	ABC University XYZ University
	Architecture firms	Head of operations	HOK
	Engineering Firms	Office manager	XYZ
Proportional spacing (best quality)	Lawyers	Managing partner CEO, CFO	ABC Law Firm DEF Law Firm
	Executives		AU
Wide documents	Accounting firms	President; CFO in corporations	Accounting

Table 4.2
Matching Differentiators to Industries Worksheet

Differentiators or Areas of Success	Person, Industry, Application	Title of Person to Contact	Companies or Applications or Departments

R.E.A.L. TIPS AND REMINDERS

☑ Before you do anything, including starting your business, you should understand where you have the greatest opportunity for success. Understand how your product is different from others, and what would be the ideal profile of a customer. If you are already in business, look at your installed base and see where the company or product has been successful.

☑ After you do this, create a calendar or plan for yourself on how and when you will actively target these industries, accounts, or applications.

☑ Set S.M.A.R.T. (specific, measurable, aligned, realistic, timed) goals and priorities to determine where you should spend your time and energy.

☑ Get up early every morning to read the paper or use the Internet to tell you what is happening situationally in your territory and industry. You will find things that you can call prospects about.

☑ Pick one business magazine to keep you abreast of what is happening in the world of business. Also read the business section of your newspaper or subscribe to the *Wall Street Journal* or *New York Times* (paper or online).

☑ Use the Internet to have it "push" information to you about companies and industries that are experiencing the issues your products or services best address. Find websites and blogs that directly relate to your choices. Google Alerts is great for this.

☑ Communicate your product or service as a solution that none of your competition can offer.

☑ Modify your standard literature or web information to reflect your unique capabilities and strengths.

☑ Test a different industry or application every quarter or $1/2$ year to see if they yield lots of opportunities.

5

Prospecting: Gaining Access to Power

ACCESS TO POWER

Let me start by saying this second stage of the sales process, prospecting, and gaining access to power, is the "hard" part of selling. It is hard because it requires a lot of time and effort (intelligent, well-focused time and effort). It is hard because there is a lot of rejection and you hear "no" a lot more than "yes." It is hard because it is repetitious and can be boring (although it doesn't have to be). It is because of these reasons, and more, that people don't prospect enough and their business suffers. Ironically, it might be the most important element of selling that a salesperson or entrepreneur can do to be successful. I like to draw a parallel to people who prospected for gold during the Gold Rush. The hard part was breaking away the stone or wading in the river to find the veins of gold. They didn't just stand in one place and wait for the gold to jump out at them. Similarly, the tough part of prospecting for salespeople is to pick away at the mountain of "nos" to get to the vein of "yes."

Why Prospect?

Why should people prospect? Well besides the obvious point of making more sales, here are some others:

- Deals don't always go the way you want, so you need to constantly generate new opportunities.
- If the person to whom you are selling leaves or is promoted, you will have to start over.
- The economy goes down and people start buying less (which is happening at the time this book is being written).
- Your competitor does something that delays or kills some of your deals.
- You are much more confident at every stage of selling when you have already closed several deals and still have numerous additional opportunities.
- You will find opportunities with no or less competition because you are prospecting and they aren't.

- It is an affordable way to reach out to people.
- You find out more about what people and the competition are doing.

No Substitute for Volume

This chapter will make prospecting better and easier, but when it comes to prospecting, there is no substitute for volume. Gaining volume is done primarily through marketing (prospecting is a subset of marketing). Allow me to clarify.

Marketing is intended to attract an audience by creating awareness of your company or your offering. There are two basic kinds of marketing: branding (for general awareness) and targeted (to get to a specific group of people). Prospecting, an individual form of marketing, is more akin to targeting individuals or companies that would benefit from your offer. For example, if I were selling a new technology for the office, I might do some marketing or advertising in a magazine or website that targets that market, but prospecting would be marketing to specific companies and people in those companies that read that same magazine or visit the website.

FOUR STAGES OF PROSPECT RECEPTIVITY (OR LACK OF)

A potential customer will receive any form of your marketing/prospecting message (letter, phone call, online e-mail, etc.) in one of four stages:

1. *Legitimately Not Interested:* and never will be (like trying to sell a car to someone who doesn't even drive). These people should be excluded from your efforts but maintained in some database to be contacted much further down the road in case you start offering different services.
2. *Just Began Considering:* This is the stage where someone, for whatever reason/s, has begun to think about buying something in the category you are selling. You want to meet these people, understand their priorities, qualify how interested they really are, influence their thinking, and stay in touch with them. If their intentions are real, this is the best stage to first meet with them.
3. *Definitely Doing Something:* You need to meet these people ASAP and hope they are not too far along in their buying process. These people will be buying something, they just have to decide from whom to buy.
4. *Too Late:* These people have recently made a decision. If you had only contacted them a little earlier, you might have won some business. You should stay in touch with these people, but the potential for a near-term sale is probably remote if they just bought something similar to what you are selling.

It is because of these different stages that companies recognize the need to market constantly. It is also why YOU MUST ALWAYS PROSPECT, no matter how well you are doing. You want to get to as many people as possible in stages two and three, and avoid stage four as much as possible to make as much money as you can.

When I was twenty-two, I learned something from a friend who worked with me. We were doing well and didn't have enough time to do everything. He suggested we hire someone to prospect for us. We hired a woman and paid her three dollars an hour (this was 1976) plus a generous commission on meetings and sales. While I was out selling, she was getting me appointments to sell more. She was well worth the money we spent. To this day, when I am teaching, my assistant Rashida is prospecting to get more business.

AN EIGHT-STEP APPROACH

I have used this eight-step approach to prospecting my entire career. If you are willing to work hard, it will work for you. The eight steps are:

1. Define your Sweet Spot.
2. Create a multiprong attack.
3. Never cold call again.
4. Find different ways to contact people.
5. Get around gatekeepers.
6. Remember: three musts when they pick up the phone or read your message.
7. Anticipate and handle objections.
8. Perform appropriate follow-up.

Step 1: Define Your Sweet Spot

Define your Sweet Spot refers to defining the right accounts, demographics, or applications for your products or services. (See the last chapter.)

Step 2: Create a Multiprong Attack

Your attack should be multipronged. Find people in the best positions to contact who could benefit from your offer, not just one person. Many people can buy, or will be interested in your offer. Try several people who could benefit, regardless of whether they are actually the decision maker. They can influence decisions or guide you to the right person who is the ultimate decision maker.

I like to imagine the company I am trying to get into as a fortress, surrounded by a moat, twenty-foot walls, and guards on top of the fortress. I need to get into this fortress by any means possible (catapult, ladders, knock the fortress door down, espionage, etc.). My chances of getting in are much better if I try different approaches versus just one. For example, I might try to batter down the six-foot-thick door surrounded by a moat, while also putting ladders up the sides of the wall, using a catapult to get in, waiting till the fortress opens, sending a message, etc.

If you are selling into a company, there is always more than one person that can benefit from your offering. Let's say you are selling a technology that helps a Sales Department sell more and travel less. Well of course you would try to get to the vice president (VP) of sales, but wouldn't a CFO be interested too, since it saves money? Or wouldn't a VP of human resources (HR) be interested because it is safer? Or how about the CEO because it is a "green" way to sell and is good for the company image and a good thing to do for the corporation? Finally, the information technology (IT) department might be interested because the product you are selling is technical in nature and they are responsible for evaluating technology.

It is important at this stage not to confuse prospecting with identifying the people involved in making the buying decision or the actual decision maker. Using the example above, the people who actually make the buying decision could be IT or VP of sales, and of course, it would be best to try to talk to them first. However, at this stage we are just trying to meet with somebody who could lead us to IT or VP of sales if we can't get to them directly.

A simpler example might be this: You are selling something that helps people clean their homes faster and better. The primary person who would make this decision is the person who is responsible for keeping the house clean (the husband, for example). You try to reach that person but to no avail, so you reach out to his wife, who could listen to you and even tell you the best time to call because she wants to help her husband. Perhaps they make enough money to afford a housekeeper who might tell you how to approach them as well.

So how do you figure out who these "other people" might be? Define the benefits of your offering and you will be able to define the people you should contact. The previous chapter gave you some insight to this, but let's use the example in Table 5.1 to take it further.

One of the products I offer is sales training over the Internet so the primary beneficiary of my service is the VP of sales, but others benefit as well:

Table 5.1
Who Needs What You Have

Product	Benefits	Contact/s
Sales training over the Internet	Train partners to sell better→	Director of partner sales
	Convert leads more effectively→	VP of marketing
	Increase sales→	VP of sales
	Reduce costs→	CFO
	Train new hires faster→	Training director

As you can see, my offer can directly or indirectly benefit many people or departments, regardless of who ultimately decides on buying my offer.

As mentioned earlier, it is always best to get to the person who benefits most directly from your offer. In most instances this person either makes the decision or influences it and directs other people on what they should do. In the example above, the VP of sales might benefit the most, but because it is a product that uses the Internet, the IT department may have to get involved to make sure it works well. So the VP of sales would direct IT to help choose the best product.

Step 3: Never Cold Call Again

Create or discover legitimate reasons to call someone rather than relying upon cold calling. Connect with other people or identify events that provide the reason for your call.

Prospecting is made even harder when you "cold call"—prospecting someone who doesn't know you, isn't expecting you, may have no need of what you're selling, etc. At best, you will catch someone in a good mood when you make your pitch. At worst, the person is busy, pressured, in a bad mood, and annoyed by your call. So you must say something that they are interested in and helps them versus talk about your product or say something generic. Here is an example of a cold call for sales training, to a VP of sales who is growing and doing a lot of hiring.

> "Hello Mr. Jones. My name is Jonathan London with IPG and I have a new product that can train your people over the Internet. Can I meet with you to discuss this?"

It is cold because it focuses more on my product and, in comparison with the next "warm example," has very little to do with the person I am calling. A warm call has more of a relationship to the person you are calling and is more relevant. For example:

> "Hello Mr. Jones. My name is Jonathan London with IPG and I noticed your ads for salespeople all over the country [legitimate reason for calling]. I was hoping to discuss with you a way for your new salespeople to be more effective [benefit 1] in a much quicker [benefit 2] and less expensive [benefit 3] manner so they can sell more [benefit 4] for you and your company."

As I hope you can see, I related my service to something the person and company were experiencing, which made it more relevant or "warmer."

Technology, the Internet, and Web 2.0 applications are tremendous tools for salespeople because they allow you to discover these kinds of situations or events in a very timely way. Once you have determined in Step 1 the best industries, and/or the best applications, for your product, you can determine what information you want to search for, and in many cases, have the Internet "push" or send news to you when it occurs. One book I recommend would be *Web 2.0 and Beyond* by Tom Funk.

My company primarily uses Google Alerts (we have five other sources as well), which allows us to define the words associated with the events we want to know are happening. For example, I entered "VP of sales" and "director of training" into my Google Alerts, and every week I get announcements of new VPs being hired or promoted. I also put in the names of my existing customers and the prospects to whom I want to sell so if something happens in their companies, I will know and can call them. I even put names of people I want to call so if something happens, I can call them about it. There are many other ways of doing this including reading trade magazines and journals, newspapers, and the websites of the company to which you want to sell. There are also websites, like Yahoo Finance and industry association websites, that can give you great information.

The key is in Step 1: deciding what your "Sweet Spot" is and finding the sources of info that keep you current so you can call people with a legitimate reason. If you are unable to take the time, don't have the resources to find something "warm" for every call or are in more of a high-volume telemarketing environment, then you should take the time to identify the titles of the people you will be calling, have an idea of what they care about, and have some scripts you can use. By focusing most of your efforts on three industries or applications, this will happen faster.

For example, a VP of sales for any company would care about:

- Increasing sales
- Increasing profits
- Training new hires faster
- Training partners to sell better
- Hiring the best people
- Having a competitive advantage

A CFO for any company would care about:

- Increasing profits
- Reducing costs
- Forecasting more effectively
- Improving cash flow
- Knowing where to invest—and where to pull back

A VP of marketing for any company would care about:

- Generating more and higher quality leads
- Creating brand awareness and loyalty

- Leveraging the Internet as effectively as possible
- Managing product launches better

Identify the people you want to call, understand their concerns or priorities, and you will be able to say and discuss things they care about when you reach out to them (an easy way to do this is find a website or magazine dedicated to that industry or job responsibility. They often will tell you what the most important issues are).

> *People Who Need People:* The warmest way and most legitimate reason to call people is through referrals. One study done years ago by a company called Target Account Selling said you have a 40 to 80 percent chance (depending upon how strong the referral is) of getting to someone if you are referred.

When I founded IPG in 1994, I was told by the gentlemen with whom I started that it would take about twelve months to have enough business to meet my financial needs, which were significant. I had just gone through an amicable divorce, but I had two young kids. I also lived in an expensive part of New Jersey. When they told me that, I told them, "I quit," when I hadn't even started. Twelve months—I would never have survived. I didn't have the financial, emotional, or psychological stability and strength to last that long (all key ingredients to be an entrepreneur). I needed to reduce this twelve months significantly and the only way I knew was to call everyone I could think of that could either buy sales training or refer me to people who could buy sales training. So, I made a list of everyone I could think of from my past and present life. I thought of everyone I could remember. When I started losing steam I created categories (elementary school friends, high school and college friends, previous co-workers, bosses, customers, relationships, friends, recruiters, consultants, etc.). I even called my ex-wife and mother of my children, Cheryl.

One name I wrote down was a fellow by the name of Matt, whom I had worked with at two different companies. We had not spoken for several years, but I called him to tell him what I was doing and to ask if he knew anyone looking for sales training. Well, not only did he know someone but he had just been asked by his boss to find someone. Forty-five days later I was training seventy-three people at the Four Seasons in Houston, Texas, at list price! I reduced my ramp time from twelve months to forty-five days. Not bad. I have been using referrals for the entire fourteen years at IPG, and it has helped me get into some of the most prestigious companies in the world.

Take as much time as you need to identify all the people you know who can either buy, or refer you to someone who can buy, your products or services. Identify the person, title, phone number, and whether or not she might buy or refer you to someone who might buy. If you can, it is also very beneficial to do this as a group, division, or company exercise. Also, be willing to pay people for referrals. It is a very inexpensive way of getting great leads. (In fact, if you know anyone who needs great sales or management training, you can go to my website, www.ipgtraining.com and click on the tab "Paid Referrals." If I make a sale to the lead you provide, we will pay you a referral fee.)

Technology is also very helpful in finding referrals. At the time of this writing, companies like LinkedIn, Plaxo, MySpace, Facebook, and Classmates are some examples of where you might find who knows who to see if you can be referred. You can also do a Google search on a person's name as well as go to the website of the company he works for to see if his biography is listed. Companies like Hoover, D+B, Jigsaw, ZoomInfo, and OneSource are also very good.

Step 4: Find Different Ways to Contact People

Find different ways to contact people in positions that could use your offerings. Use the phone, letters, e-mail, fax, third-party introductions, or any other way you can find. Although you will probably use one or two primary ways to do your prospecting, be flexible and try different approaches. People are more or less receptive to different forms of communication, and it is less boring for you. You want to optimize your chances of reaching someone by choosing the right approach. Some options include:

- Phone
- Introduction
- E-mail
- Invitation (to trade shows, webinars, company or social events, etc.)
- Postcards
- Search
- Fax
- Direct mail (traditional or over web)
- Blogs or chat groups
- Web 2.0 (social networks, viral, etc.)
- FedEx, UPS, DHL, etc.

A friend of mine was prospecting for a job. He went to Monster.com and saw a job at a very big company he wanted to work for in his neighborhood. He didn't know anyone so he sent a very professionally written fax that ended up on the desk of the hiring manager. He followed that up with a phone call and got the job.

Don't be afraid to be creative. I use Evites for meetings. A student of mine told me she once sent a bag of oranges to a client with the question, "Can you squeeze me in?" Another student sent a very expensive designer shoe with a note that said, "Since I have one foot in the door, can I get the other in?" My primary method is a combination of using references or current events (things occurring to them, their company, or industry), followed up by phone and e-mail, or e-mail and phone. I occasionally use invitations to webinars or send people some info about a situation occurring in their world and comment on how we can assist them. For example, I am currently trying to sell to a large social network. I was referred to the EVP of sales by someone I had previously trained. I tried phone and e-mail with the e-mail connecting first. The EVP referred me to the person who was running the sales training project. As I am working this deal, I am using Google Alerts to keep me aware of things that are happening in this company, its industry, and with its competitors. I use these alerts to comment and show how our program will help them.

Many years ago, there was a company in the telecommunications industry doing a lot of print advertising. I took about ten of these advertisements and wrote a cover letter to the VP of sales and the VP of marketing saying how impressed I was with the advertising and wondering how efficiently the sales team was closing on the leads. I received a call from the VP of marketing to discuss how I could help close more of the leads. One of the reasons the letter worked so well was the relevancy. The other reason was that the VP of marketing and VP of sales each wanted to have the upper hand on the other. (This is called company politics and is a very powerful lever to pull.)

As I have already mentioned, my first years in sales I was selling typewriters. I also sold calculators and eventually word processors (when they were separate machines costing over fifteen thousand dollars). I sent a hanging folder to prospects, the kind you probably have in your desk today, with a tab that said Olivetti. My initial letter was clipped to the outside of the folder telling my prospects that I would occasionally be sending them information about my offerings and if they were interested to call me. If not, they could just put the information in the folder for future reference. This gave me an advantage when people needed something because they thought of me, or took my call when I called them, or let me in when I dropped by their office. I had them covered in Stage 2 (Just Began Considering) and Stage 3 (Definitely Doing Something). You can do this today by asking people to make a folder in their e-mail for them to put your marketing materials in.

Today, the web, search engines, your website, social networks, widgets, and business or social networks (commonly referred to as Web 2.0) must be a substantive part of your approach. You can buy e-mail lists, which allow you to do direct marketing electronically. You can optimize your website for the key words people use when they are interested in services you and your competition offer (this is called SEO or search engine optimization). You can enter keywords into any search engine (Google, Yahoo, and Microsoft being the biggest at the time of this writing) and pay only when a person clicks on one of your ads (my wife, Puja, at www.pujahall.com, is a psychoanalyst and is building her practice this way). You can also control your budget and decide how much or how little each of those clicks is worth. Most companies offer people who come to their site something of value (case studies, white papers, newsletters, etc.) and more if people are willing to give them some contact information (the minimum being their names and e-mail addresses) that you can use to remarket to them.

One of my best clients uses a technology that lets them know when people come to the company's website. When this happens, a person will greet and qualify their interest over the web by chatting with them. Once this is done (if the prospect has allowed them) a salesperson will call them to see if they can sell them something. It is a very successful model. There is a multitude of ways to find people that are interested in your offering. Find the best ones for you and use them.

Step 5: Get Around Gatekeepers

Find ways to get around the human and the technology gatekeepers. What is a gatekeeper? A gatekeeper is anyone that prevents you from getting to the person you wish to speak with. It is also any technology, like voicemail or answering machines, that screen your efforts, or spam filters in e-mail that look at your e-mail and decide if the e-mail should go through to the intended person. Getting around these is a lot of fun and takes creativity and ingenuity. There are several ways to get around each. Although these work well, none works all the time, so you need to try different techniques depending upon your situation.

Personal or administrative assistants (PA or AA) are trained to keep you away. A PA once told me her bonuses were based on how few people got to her boss. Some effective ways around these people are

- Call when the gatekeeper is least likely to be there, which is early in the day, late in the day, or around lunch.
- Use a referral: it is highly improbable for an assistant to keep you out if you were referred by someone. This does not guarantee you will get an appointment, but it does increase the odds significantly (up to 80 percent if it is a strong referral).
- Send an e-mail to the prospect: most people check their own e-mails.
- Ask for the gatekeeper's help and guidance.
- Tell the gatekeeper you will call back when the person you want to speak with is available and ask when that might be (or do this first and then say you will call back).
- If the call is personal in nature, say that and ask when the prospect will be back.

The biggest gatekeeper today in the business world is voice-mail. It has become one of the biggest roadblocks in gaining access to people. There are several ways to deal with this. First, leave a professional voicemail with a sense of intrigue. For example, if you were calling someone in an industry you had done work with before, you might say, "Hello Mr./Ms. Smith, my name is Joe Herman and I am calling because of the recent work we did with a competitor (or mention the name of the company) in your industry and, without sharing confidences, I would like to get your thoughts and insights. Please give me a call at your earliest convenience at...."

Another example would be to reference the warm reason from Step 2. "Mr. Smith, my name is Joe Herman with XYZ and I just read the speech you gave and want to ask you a few questions. Please call me at...." Even if he doesn't call back, the next time you call if your message was interesting enough, he will be a bit more curious and take your call. Other ways of dealing with voicemail are:

- "0" out to get the companywide receptionist and ask for the person.
- "0" out and ask for the president or a high-level executive's office and then ask to be transferred once you speak to someone. Being transferred from a higher authority will also get attention.
- Tell the person to be looking for a special e-mail or package you are sending. (Make sure you send it.)
- Don't leave a message at all, ever. Some people think this is better, but I think it is more appropriate when you have already left several messages and don't want to be bothering someone.
- Tell the person if she gives you five minutes and is not interested after that, you will never call again.

If e-mail is your primary mode of prospecting, here are some ways to avoid being put into junk mail (there are lots of companies that help you do this and I would advise you using or consulting with one):

- Use the name of the company you are prospecting in the subject line.
- Use re: or fw:
- Use the prospect's name in the subject line.
- Don't use words such as *free* or *special* in the subject line.
- Avoid any attachments including your company logo if it is part of your signature and could be seen as an attachment.

Step 6: Remember: Three Musts When They Pick up the Phone or Read Your Message

When you reach this stage, three things must happen quickly once a person answers the phone, reads your letter, or opens his or her e-mail. First, you must establish immediate credibility and interest. Next, you must present two to three benefits as early in the call as possible (this increases your odds significantly). Third, you must request an appointment or ask for some action you want taken. *Always:*

- Prepare before you make a call.
- Keep your comments short and sweet.
- Be yourself and use a conversational tone (if on the phone).
- Be ready for resistance, objections, and know how you will respond.

Never:

- Sound canned or scripted.
- Be vague or use acronyms the person won't understand.
- Be arrogant or upset because they never called you back.

> Sample: A Call to a VP of Sales at an International Company
> "Good morning, Mr./Ms. Jones. My name is Sam Smith with Acme. I am calling at the suggestion of Andrew Wilson [**instant credibility**]. I hope this is a good time.
>
> Andrew suggested I call due to our recent success at his company [**more credibility**]. He thought our solutions might help you in the same way by:
>
> - Expanding your business by finding more partners to sell your product [**benefit 1**].
> - Reducing your operating costs by up to 20 percent using our technology [**benefit 2**].
> - Increasing your close ratios and selling bigger deals by training your people [**benefit 3.**]
>
> Do you have some time in the next few weeks for us to meet?"

Ways to Establish Credibility Quickly

A reference is always the best way to establish credibility because it immediately breaks down barriers. Think about it—if someone were to call you and mention the name of someone you like, know, or trust, your natural demeanor would probably be less guarded and more open to giving the person calling a few seconds to speak and hear what she has to say.

The second best way is to use the suggestions made in Step 3 of this chapter. Find events that are occurring to them personally, in people's company, industry, competitors, or in society as a whole (At the time of this writing the economy is a big concern, so people would respond to that.)

Titles also establish credibility. If you are focusing on a particular industry or application you can call yourself a "specialist." ("I am the legal specialist for ...") Or if you are the only person responsible for a certain area, you can call yourself "dedicated." (I am the dedicated person for your account.)

Mentioning the competition or something the other person would know will also establish credibility. Using the legal example again, if you had done or are doing some work for another firm you could say "I just did some work for Crane, Blame, and Explain," which would be a name they would know. If you are selling a consumer product, you can do the same thing by mentioning other people in their neighborhood who have bought the same thing.

Statistics are also very powerful at this stage. If you can mention a percentage that is relevant early on, people will be more open. For example, "Hello Mr. Jones, my name is ... and I am calling because 18 percent of our customers are ..."

Table 5.2
Sample Benefits to a CFO

Title	Benefits of Sales Training
CFO	*Increase profits* by teaching your people how to negotiate more effectively.
	Reduce costs by making them more productive faster and having your channels sell more.
	Better forecasting which allows the CFO a better control of the business.
	Improved cash flow by selling to creditworthy customers.

Present Two to Three Benefits to Prospects as Early in the Call as Possible

Benefits are what the person gets from your product or service. Without benefits, prospects don't know why they should do what you are asking them to do. The reason you need to express two or three benefits is the one you mention may not be the one they care about. Also, giving the person more than one benefit has a cumulative effect and has more of an impact.

Going back to the example above, there are three benefits offered to the VP of International Sales:

- *Expanding* your business by finding more partners to sell your product **[benefit 1]**.
- *Reducing* your operating costs by up to 20 percent using our technology **[benefit 2]**.
- *Increasing* your close ratios and selling bigger deals by training your people **[benefit 3]**.

Do you know which words are the benefit words? Those that are in italic. Benefits address people's concerns. Table 5.2 is an example of how sales training can benefit a CFO.

Use Table 5.3 below and/or a piece of paper to outline the benefits of your offer to the different people you will be calling. Remember, the more specific the better. If you have numbers and percentages that are real, use them. They are objective proof and carry a lot of weight.

Close for an Action

Close is a word salespeople use that reflects the process of getting some-body to do something. Usually you hear it in the sense of "close the sale," but it can also be used when you want a prospect to take action in some way. There are many actions you might want prospects to take after you give them your benefit statement. The most common is to meet with you, but others can include:

- Seeing a demo.
- Going to your website.

Table 5.3
Outline Your Benefits to Your Prospects

Title of Person	Concerns, Issues, Goals	Your Benefits

- Attending a seminar or webinar.
- Filling out a survey.
- Entering a contest.
- Introducing you to others.

Using E-mail to Prospect

Sending an e-mail to prospects is very similar to the steps already described. You need to get people's attention, say something that benefits them, and ask them to take an action. It is a great medium to prospect since it is the primary way of communications in almost every company. It is also easier to respond to or forward than voicemail. Yes it is also easy to delete, but so is a voicemail. Let's break down the components.

Subject Line.   The subject line is what gets attention. The trick here is to convert what you would have said on the phone into a subject line that grabs people. I was teaching this concept to one of my clients and asked him to send an e-mail over lunch to a prospect they were having difficulty reaching. The prospect was neck and neck for being number one in his industry. He came back from lunch and told everyone he got the appointment. When we asked him what his subject line was, he told us "Kick Company X's Behind and Take More Market Share." It was a bit brazen, and I wouldn't recommend it as your first gambit, but it proves the point. It got the prospect's attention and was highly relevant. Table 5.4 shows some more conventional examples of taking what you would have said on the phone and making it a subject line in an e-mail.

Make sure your subject line doesn't sound too general. It won't stand out and will probably get put into their junk mail. Also, if you can find a way to put your prospect's company name in the subject line, it probably won't get put into junk mail.

Benefits in an E-mail.   People should see your introduction and the benefits to them in their preview pane. They should not have to open the e-mail entirely to see whether they want to go further. We call this the "no scroll

Table 5.4
Converting a Credibility Statement to a Subject Line on E-mail

Credibility statement on phone	Subject line in an e-mail
Joe Jones told me to call	Joe Jones told me to call
I am calling about your recent promotion	Your recent promotion
I am calling about your new product release	Sell more of product XYZ
Recent work we did in your industry	Recent work we did with company XYZ

rule." Just by previewing your e-mail, they should be enticed. Bullets versus paragraphs should always be used, and you should highlight (in bold, or underscore) the key words you want them to pay attention to. Here is an example (the border represents the preview screen):

Hi Greg,

My name is David Schmidt, and I'm the dedicated Account Manager for XYZ Corp. Art Rumf suggested that I speak with you to see how we could help your service-and-support team:

1. **Identify problems** before they occur to save you money.
2. **Improve visibility** to production issues for better customer satisfaction.
3. Identify and **solve problems faster** to make more money.

How can we get on your calendar to discuss further? I will call to see when you have some time or just reply to let me know.

Dave

Step 7: Anticipate and Handle Objections

Unfortunately, no matter how well you execute the steps already outlined, you will still get resistance and objections. The best way to handle objections is to anticipate them and say something before the person you are calling can verbalize it. For example, if you were calling someone you knew was using a competitor, you could say, "Hi, my name is.... and I am calling because I know you are a happy user of...." This minimizes the odds of the person using it against you as an objection. ("We already use XYZ to manage that.") More likely you will get an answer like "That's right," or "Yes we are," which allows you to go on with your benefit statement. Another example might be this: You have tried getting to someone many times. Finally, he picks up the phone. You could say, "Hi, my name is.... and I know you are busy so I will be brief." There are more objections than you think that could be handled in this way.

The second best way to handle objections is to follow this rule: Acknowledge the objection and then say or ask something to get a response. Using the same examples as above without knowing beforehand, if a prospect said she was happy with your competition, you could say, "That is great. Our program is extremely complementary and actually makes your program better." Or if she said she was extremely busy, you could say, "I'm glad to hear that because that is why I am calling. I can help you get more done in the same time. Can we speak?" Here are some ways of acknowledging an objection:

- "Thanks for your candor."
- "I appreciate that."
- "I understand."
- "That is to be expected."
- "A lot of my customers have told me that."
- "We are hearing that a lot."
- "Sorry to hear that."
- "No problem."

Different things you can say or ask are:

- "That is why I am calling."
- "That is why we should meet."
- "That is exactly why our customers do business with us."

Putting both of these elements together would sound like this:

- "I appreciate your candor and that is exactly why I was calling."
- "I understand, which is why I was hoping to meet."

Below is a list of common objections and how to handle them. Using the table below as a guideline, list the most common or difficult objections and write down how you could anticipate or handle them.

I Use a Competitor:
- Anticipate: "I am calling because I believe you are currently using ..."
- Acknowledge/say or ask: "No problem. We work with them all the time. What are you using them for?"

There is No Budget/Money:
- Anticipate: "I am calling because I imagine at this time budgets are low or nonexistent. Is that true?"

- Acknowledge, say, or ask: "I am sorry to hear that, but that is why I am calling," or, "Most of my recent customers have said the same thing. May I ask what your situation is? Perhaps we can meet to see if we can help."

I'm Happy with Our Current Vendor:
- Anticipate: "That is why I was calling. We have been having tremendous success working with ...," or, "We have a program that is extremely complementary to your current vendor's."
- Acknowledge, say, or ask: "That's good because it means you appreciate the benefits of this type of product or service. How long have you been using it?" or "Which version or how much of their offering are you using."

Send Me Information:
- Anticipate: N/A
- Acknowledge, say, or ask: "I would be happy to. What would you like me to send and when can we discuss it?" Or, "Before I send you info that may be irrelevant to you, can I ask why you want me to send you info and what you are most interested in?" Or, "Of course. How many sets would you like or who will you be sharing this with?" Or, "Can I assume this means you are interested? When can we meet or talk to discuss this?" Or, "Do you have a few minutes now? I can show you on our website." Or, "How would you like to try it instead of just read about it?" Or, "We don't have literature, just me who can answer and ask questions." Or, "If you are at all interested, I will be in your area or available [give a date and time]. Does that work for you?"

You Should Speak with (Someone Else or with Less Authority):
- Anticipate: "I was calling you because nobody else in your organization has the information you do." Or, "I was calling you to get your insights." Or, "I know I will need to work with someone else, but can you give me your thoughts before I do so I am prepared?"
- Acknowledge, say, or ask: "I appreciate that. What is that person's role?" Or, "I appreciate that. What should I discuss with him?" Or, "I appreciate that but that is the responsibility of someone else on my team. I am responsible for working at your level."

We will go into greater depth on handling objections in Chapter 8.

Step 8: Perform Appropriate Follow-Up

If you are prospecting on the phone or e-mail to a specific person, then following up (calling to try and get to someone) two to three times per week for the first few weeks is okay. A good friend of mine says she has no limit. She will chase them down till she gets to them because she believes so much in her product. If after a few weeks you have not spoken with or received a response to any of your messages, it is probably a good time to also start reaching out to others who can benefit from your product or service.

If you are using e-mail as more of a mass marketing or direct mail tool to create awareness, then depending on your product, once a week or once a month is a good rule of thumb. You can punctuate this schedule with anything that is relevant to the prospect. Send the mailings at a time when people are more likely to open it (weekends or holidays when it is less busy for them, early in the day, etc.). Make it interesting or people will "unsubscribe" from your mailing list.

How Much Should You Prospect?

Table 5.5 provides an example to determine how much you should prospect every month/week/day:

Table 5.5
How Much You Should Prospect

Step 1 - Determine monthly target or quota.	$500,000
Step 2 - Determine average sale size.	50,000
Step 3 - Determine number of sales you need to make a month by dividing Step 1 by Step 2.	$500,000/$50,000 = 10 sales per month
Step 4 - What is your closing % on deals from first meetings?	25%
Step 5 - Calculate number of first meetings you need to have based on close rate.	40 first meetings × 25% Close Rate = 10 sales
Step 6 - Number of contacts, calls, etc., you need to get a meeting multiplied by the number of first meetings required in Step 5.	25 attempts × 40 meetings = 1,000 attempts
Step 7 - Average number of minutes each attempt takes multiplied by number of attempts, broken down into hours/month.	3 minutes × 1,000 attempts = 3,000 minutes/60 = 50 hours per month
Step 8 - Calculate number of hours per week and day you need to prospect.	50 hours per month/4 weeks = 12.5 hours/5 days = 2.5 hours a day

You can spend less time prospecting by:

- Improving your close rates.
- Increasing your deal size.
- Using seminars, webinars, and other forms of marketing to reach people versus just the phone, e-mail, etc.
- Using references as much as possible.
- Selling to your base of accounts once you have them.

It might be helpful to use the prospecting form, as shown in Table 5.6.

Table 5.6
Prospecting Form

PROSPECTING FORM
Who are you calling:
What will be your credibility statement?
_____
What are your three reasons or benefits to the customer?
1. _____
2. _____
3. _____
What questions and objections do you anticipate? How will you handle?
1. _____
2. _____
3. _____
How will you close for the appointment?
_____
_____
_____

CATEGORIZING YOUR OPPORTUNITIES

Once you get a list of prospects using the method just outlined, you'll need to prioritize them. Where should you spend the most time and effort? Look at your list and determine the business potential they represent. What is your estimated value for the products and services you could provide? Put your prospects in one of three categories—A, B, or C. The bulleted points will help you determine where to put prospects. Although you should spend most of your time prospecting A-level opportunities, B- and C-level prospects are sometimes worth pursuing.

Group A. The Best

- Highly visible or strategic.
- You have a relationship with them.
- They value you and you have a strategic relationship.
- You can use them as a reference.
- You are knowledgeable about their industry or requirements.
- They are a good fit to your company's offerings.
- High revenue potential for you.
- You are the sole provider in your category.
- Application fit is excellent.
- A partner of yours has a strong relationship with them.
- They are a company that is growing.
- Potential exists for long-term business.
- Other? (geographic proximity, good industry for you, etc.)

Group B. Second Best

- If a customer, they are satisfied, but not as strategic or well known as Group A.
- You share the business with a competitor/s.
- Smaller annual potential.
- There may be additional business for you and your company, but it will take effort to dig it out.
- The customer is a good reference and a testimonial letter is possible.
- May not have the same volume potential as an A-level prospect, but possibly a shorter sales cycle.
- Partner has a strong relationship with them.
- Other?

Group C. Third Best

- A small customer with limited potential.
- You and your company are probably a second or third source.
- Additional business potential is minimal.
- You and your company have not been able to gain a solid foothold within the account.

- You may still be proving the value of its products and services.
- You would not ask for a testimonial or use as a reference.
- Level-C prospects should only be called on in the absence of A- or B-level prospects.

REAL TERRITORY AND ACCOUNT MANAGEMENT

Following are some tools you can use to manage your time and increase your sales opportunities.

Your Top Opportunities

Based upon the criteria in the last few pages, use Table 5.7 to list and rank the top prospects in your territory. You can make this bigger or

Table 5.7
List and Rank Your Accounts

Rank A, B, C	Account Name	New Business Potential for 12 Months	Why and How?
A	The Big Company	$500,000	Solution A—call
B	A Pretty Big Company	$250,000	Solution B—invite to webinar
C	A Smaller Company	$25,000	Solution C—call; need to pay the bills

Table 5.8
Make Time to Prospect

TIME	MONDAY	TUESDAY	WEDNESDAY	THURSDAY	FRIDAY	SATURDAY	SUNDAY
7 AM							
8 AM	Industry 1—A Accounts		Industry 2—A Accounts		Industry 3—A Accounts	Send e-mails to executives	Rest
9 AM	→		→		→		
10 AM							
11 AM							
12 AM							
1 PM							
2 PM							
3 PM							
4 PM							
5 PM	Industry 1—B Accounts		Industry 2—B Accounts		Industry 3—B Accounts		
6 PM	→		→		→		

smaller depending on what you are selling or how many people you have on your sales team.

TOP PROSPECT LIST

IMPLEMENTING YOUR PLAN

Now that you have identified your plan, you must execute it. To do so most effectively, you should integrate the activities involved into your daily and weekly structure. Table 5.8 is an example of how to fill in your calendar with specific times to prospect.

R.E.A.L. TIPS AND REMINDERS

☑ The first thing people respond to on the phone is the tone and quality of your voice. People want to work with people they trust and who they feel are genuine. Therefore, it is not only what you say but also your attitude, tone of voice, and your intention when making the call that important.

☑ There is tremendous resistance around prospecting. It is the hard work of selling and most people avoid it, but it is the most important thing for you to do to grow your business and be a confident salesperson.

☑ Depending on what you are selling, your call might be the most important call your prospects take that day. If it leads to a sale, it might be the most important thing they do and help others, so don't undervalue your call.

☑ Prospecting is a numbers game. Don't get frustrated when most of your efforts yield nothing. Using the system discussed in this chapter will increase your performance, but you will still hear "no" more often than "yes."

☑ Don't take it personally. Be thick skinned. Just keep doing it. You will get results.

☑ You need to be patient. Don't expect immediate results and have confidence that all will work out for the best if you just keep doing the right thing. Prospecting is hard. Don't quit.

☑ If you can, work in an environment that doesn't distract you.

☑ Use of benefit words like *control, prosper, enhance, reduce, and save*, etc., appeals to people and will create action. Studies say that use of three of these words together increases your odds to sell something by 64 percent.

☑ Use the Internet to understand what is most current and relevant in their world so you can say something that is of most interest to them.

☑ Play the Name Game. List all the people from your life that you can remember, past and present (K-12, college, previous employers, co-workers, bosses, customers, prospects, current people in same categories, headhunters, venture capitalists, your accountant, lawyer, people you play ball with, friends, and more). Decide if they can either buy what you are selling or refer you to someone who can.

☑ Make a time every day that is the best (usually early and late) so that you, and the people you are calling won't feel hurried.

☑ Send e-mails so they are received on weekends when the inbox is less crowded.

☑ Mix it up. Think of prospecting like marketing. Message people in different ways. Give yourself a little variety so it is less tedious.

☑ Hire someone to do it for you and pay them more on results than effort. The better they are, the more you both make.

☑ There are many online technologies that can make your marketing materials look as good as the largest organizations in the world. Use them.

☑ Use the prospecting approach taught in this chapter. We have been using it at IPG for fourteen years, and it has gotten us into some of the largest accounts in the world.

☑ If a person says he is not interested, ask him if he knows someone who might be.

☑ If you are using a customer relationship management tool, enter the names of all the companies you want to sell to and modify the fields to show the titles of the people you would like to get to (at the beginning these will be empty but should fill up over time).

☑ If you are just starting, you are allowed to eat, sleep, pray, and be with your loved ones—the rest of your time should be spent prospecting.

6

Qualifying Prospects and Discovering Needs

Your prospecting has paid off and you got an appointment. Nice work! But now what? You have one chance, and you don't want to blow it. The S.PRI.N.G. Dialogue is a very effective way to help salespeople differentiate themselves in the eyes of the prospect and get more information, which is crucial to winning as many sales opportunities as possible. S.PRI.N.G. stands for Situation, Priorities, Needs (theirs and yours), and Gain.

Most salespeople would say that the sale is made when you present or demonstrate your solution. Although it is true that you need to be good at this stage of the sale, your effectiveness is directly aligned with how well you have qualified an opportunity and how much information you have. Getting information is a big challenge because salespeople don't know what to ask and how to ask, and they have to get through the resistance and mistrust people have of them. More often than necessary, a sale begins or sinks into an adversarial situation in which both sides (especially the prospect) feel the need to protect themselves. Prospects don't tell salespeople what they want to know, and for good reason. Stories abound where salespeople take advantage and sell the wrong thing, so prospects are wary. In turn, salespeople start to push their agenda too hard and turn the prospect off. Because the prospect's guard is up, it is difficult for the professional, well-intended salesperson to gain the information needed to recommend the proper product or solution.

Fortunately, if you do the things we discussed in previous chapters, you will have already created a better scenario in which to sell, especially if you are selling to your Sweet Spot and got the appointment via a reference or a current event. Using the S.PRI.N.G. Dialogue, prospects will tell you more and be more receptive to things you tell them. It will help you "qualify" your prospect, which is to say, understand two critical things as early as possible:

- Is there a sales opportunity that you can win?
- Should you walk away because there is very little, or no chance to win?

Several years ago, I was going on my first sales call as Regional Director with one of my sales reps, Karen, to sell some videoconferencing equipment to Warren, the buyer at a division of one of the world's largest healthcare companies. According to Karen, Warren was not a nice person. From what I was told, we were two diametrically opposed forces in suits: Good and Evil (I was the good one of course).

I had just returned from a week's meditation retreat and was in a very mellow and peaceful space. You can call it relaxed. I would call it calm, happy, very present, content, and not worried or anxious. I was very aware that I was a regional director, responsible for helping my people sell video-conferencing, but I was not feeling pressured by it. Nor was I fearful of Warren. What happened was quite remarkable. Karen and I sat in front of Warren's big macho desk, and Karen introduced me. I just began to talk to Warren. I asked about him, his position, what was important to him, what he wanted to have happen by using videoconferencing, what he wanted to avoid, what were the many reasons driving his requirements, what success or failure looked like, etc. It was as if his desk disappeared. Warren let down his guard and was not the ogre Karen had portrayed. He actually came out from behind his desk to sit with Karen and me. Why? Because he was responding to my manner, and the focus on him and what he cared about. He felt safe. It was an incredible meeting, and we got the deal thirty days later (the normal sales cycle was six months or longer).

Conversely, there have been times when I have met someone and knew there was no chance of winning the business. Again as a director selling videoconferencing, I remember going out on a call with one of my reps to a large insurance company. Afterwards, while we were in the taxi I asked him how he thought it went. He told me he thought it went well, and I bet him twenty dollars that we would not win. He looked at me like I was crazy because I was his manager and I was supposed to positive and confident. He still owes me twenty dollars.

MASTERING AND USING SALES TOOLS

The greatest professionals in any endeavor have mastered their tools, which provide a higher quality and quantity of results. For example, in golf, a driver is basically the same for everybody. But Tiger Woods can make a driver do more things in more situations because he has mastered the tool. He also takes the same stance and uses the same process to approach the ball so he consistently performs better than his competition (sorry, Phil Mickelson). An artist is the same way. In my hands I can hardly paint a wall while an artist creates a masterpiece. The S.PRI.N.G Dialogue is a tool that any entrepreneur or salesperson would do well to master. It will:

- Differentiate you in a very positive way so the prospect feels better with you than with your competition.
- Help you feel more prepared for an initial meeting with anyone, in any situation. Provide a structure that allows for deviations or detours in a call but still allows you to get the information you need.

- Help you win more sales.
- Put you in the upper echelons of sales professionals.
- Reduce barriers.
- Increase trust.
- Help you get more information so you can sell more effectively.
- Help reveal larger opportunities via effective questioning.

S.PRI.N.G. Dialogue

Let's take a close look at the S.PRI.N.G. Dialogue:

Situation: This is the beginning of your interaction, so the "S" means understanding a little about the prospect's current situation. It also means getting off to a good *START* by asking good questions and showing prospects you have done a little homework about their company, industry, or even the individual (without invading their privacy). You also begin to read their DiSC style and make them comfortable in this segment.

Priorities: These are the reasons people have agreed to talk/meet with you: to see if there is a way that you can help them with their priorities and resolve their problems. Depending upon with whom you are speaking, priorities can be many things including goals, challenges, issues, projects, areas of focus, problems, etc. You should use this part of the dialogue to understand why these are priorities, what has caused them to be so, and what the impact of success or failure around these priorities has for them individually, for their department, and for the company as a whole. Specific monetary figures should be uncovered so you can more easily justify your offering. This is also a time you can begin to start planting seeds or criteria for your solution that will help influence the deal in your favor. A "seed" is something about you, your company, your product, or your experience that addresses something the prospect has said (more will be discussed later in this chapter).

Needs: This part of the dialogue has two purposes. The first is to inquire further about, or suggest ideas regarding what they need to do to address their priorities and resolve their problems. The second part is to discover what you need to know to win the deal: questions about the competition, decision process, politics, budget, decision criteria, and more to develop effective strategies. These are questions you can't ask until you've earned the right to by going through the previous steps. If you do, you'll get shut out. You also continue to plant seeds here to influence their thinking and formal criteria.

Gain: Most important, use the dialogue to uncover a business and personal win or gain for them, to help them get what they want, or avoid what they don't want, and to have them see and associate you with these wins. This is crucial because it is the most personal reason they will take action (and thus the reason you ask it last). Being able to address personal issues will help you win more sales.

Preparing for the S.PRI.N.G. Dialogue

Great salespeople go into a sales call prepared by researching the company, person, and or industry with whom they are meeting beforehand. They will plot what information they want to get, questions they want to ask, and anything else they want to have happen in a meeting and what a good next step or steps would be to make a sale. Below is an example of a list of questions that you might ask at a meeting (your list will be different, of course, based on your products and the unique selling situation):

- Who do the prospects currently use as the vendor?
- What are they happy or not happy with?
- What is their motivation for this meeting?
- Whom do they consider the competition?
- What challenges or obstacles do they see in being successful?
- What are the financial gains of success or the consequences of failure?
- Who is involved in making a decision?
- What is their time line?
- What is their budget?
- What criteria will they use in making a decision?
- Who else will they be considering?

As mentioned above, great salespeople also define what else they want to have happen in the meeting, and how they should prepare. Questions to kick-start your thinking here include:

- How will you start the meeting?
- What do you want to tell the prospect?
- How will you make a good impression?
- What do you want to have happen as an outcome of the meeting?
- What would be the next best step?
- Who should you bring with you?
- What materials should you hand out?
- Who will be attending on the prospect's side?
- Do you need a laptop and PowerPoint presentation?
- How should you modify the presentation for the prospect?
- How should you dress?
- Should you go alone or with someone to support you?

Finally, a good salesperson will do some research. You should search for information, including:

- Information about the company and persons with whom you are meeting.
- Current events or press releases about the company.
- Whether you or your company has sold anything to another company in that industry.

- Whether you know someone at the company. Do you know anyone who knows the person you are meeting at the company?
- Some industry trends and acronyms you can use to convey the impression that you are an insider.
- Current financials (earnings, profits, growth) of the prospect.
- 10K or annual reports to understand more financial details.

The easiest, fastest, and most abundant way to do all this is via the Internet, specifically:

- Using Google or other search engines to search on the company or person with whom you are meeting.
- Going to the company's website to look up the bios of the people with whom you are meeting.
- Reviewing any recent press releases.
- Using services such as Hoovers, ZoomInfo, OneSource, LinkedIn, or others to find out about the major competitors of the prospect.
- Finding industry-specific websites.
- Going into your own database to see if you have done any work with the person, company, or in the industry of the company you are meeting with.
- Doing it the old fashioned way via magazines, newspapers, library visit, etc., or talking to people who might know something to help you prepare.

S.PRI.N.G. DIALOGUES: SITUATION AND START

Starting off a meeting well can pave the way toward a sale. But go slowly.

I remember once doing some research on a gentleman from Sprint I had never met. I looked up his bio on its website and found out he went to the University of Maryland the same time I went to American University. After saying thanks for his time, I mentioned my research and asked him if he was into basketball. We talked about basketball for fifteen minutes and then started the business conversation. Needless to say, he was very open to talking and sharing things with me.

With another prospect I mentioned some trends I was observing in her industry (software). She thought it was an interesting subject and one near and dear to her heart. We had a good S.PRI.N.G. Dialogue.

Situation and Start

This is the beginning and also tends to be the shortest segment of the dialogue (it could/should go a little longer with prospects who are more people oriented—the Influential and Steadfast behavior styles). The prospect's initial impression of you begins here. Depending upon his mood, experience, DiSC style, how you got the appointment, etc., he may be more or less patient or receptive (Dominants are very impatient) or judgmental (Ds and Cs are the most critical and judgmental). It is imperative to get off to a good start by making a good impression on the people you are meeting with. You want them to feel like this will be different and more interesting than other meetings they have had with other salespeople. If so, they will be more willing to tell you things, and they will be more receptive to what you say to them.

Making a good impression can be done many ways, including:

- Confirming the appointment and agenda before you arrive.
- Demonstrating your awareness and/or expertise of their company or industry early in the dialogue.
- Asking interesting questions.
- Creating good rapport quickly.
- Reading their DiSC style and adapting as quickly as possible so they are comfortable with you.
- Having a clever ice breaker.
- Wearing or using something from their company.
- Being real, relaxed, prepared, and confident.
- Simply being well rounded, interested, interesting, and truly focused on and appreciative of the time you are with the prospect.

Some examples would be:

"Thank you for your time today, I know how busy you must be. My intention in the time we have is to understand the most important things you wish to achieve, as well as prevent, and to see if my company can help. I'll also make sure you know about what we do and answer any questions you might have. Would that be OK?"

"Thank you for agreeing to spend time with me today to discuss your priorities and needs. Today, I would like to find out a little more about your organization and priorities. From there, I can be as specific as possible in describing my company, our approach, and how we can help."

"I know you are anxious to hear about my company, but I would like to tell you within a context more specific to you, so may I ask you some questions?"

"Before we discuss finance, technology, etc., I would like to understand your overall business goals and objectives. Is that OK with you?"

"Before we start, I want to say I use your product and I think it is fantastic."

"I want to confirm we have X amount of time and review the agenda I sent, including a brief overview of my company. Then we'll turn the focus on you and your company. Does that work for you?

"Thanks for having me. You shared with me that you have about thirty minutes. Is this still OK? Great. What I would like to do with the time is start with you and then make sure we have time to answer all your questions and tell you about my company."

"Thank you for agreeing to spend time with me today to discuss your priorities and needs. Today, I would like to find out a little more about your organization and priorities. From there, I can be specific as possible in describing our approach and how we might help."

"I know you are anxious to hear about my company and I want to tell you, but I would like to tell you within a context more specific to you. So may I ask you some questions?"

"Before we discuss all the technical elements of your requirement or RFP and our solution, I would like to understand the bigger picture ..."

"As my organization does several things, including [mention them], I would like to understand a bit more about what you are looking for so I can focus on the service of most interest. May I ask some questions?"

Exercise: Think of a prospect you will be meeting with soon. How will you begin your dialogue? What will you say or do to show them that you are different than other salespeople and to engage them early? Get out a piece of paper and script your opening comments, tailored to the person and situation.

Another way to set the right tone is to demonstrate how much you have prepared by bringing your research into the conversation as early as possible. The more you do so, the better the entire interaction will be. You can do this either before or after you set, or confirm, the agenda for the meeting.

Some of the items you might mention are:

- Information about the company and people.
- Current events or press releases about the company.
- Some industry research including trends.
- Current financials (earnings, profits, growth) of the prospect.
- Information in their 10K or annual reports to understand more financial details.

Finally, the easiest and most common way (but not best because this is what most salespeople do) of starting a meeting is to mention something you see in their office or something general: a picture on their wall, the weather, a recent news event (not political or religious), etc.

Here are some examples of how you can bring all of this together at the beginning or "S" of a S.PRI.N.G. Dialogue:

Opening: "Thank you for your time today, I know how busy you must be. My intention in the time we have is to understand what are the most important things you wish to achieve, and avoid, and to see if I and my company can help. Would that be OK?"

Fact Confirmation: "I noticed that your sales are growing faster than your competitor's. Congratulations! How are you doing that? What elements do you wish to continue?

My research says your company currently does about X million per year and are located in sixteen cities. Is that correct? Can you tell me a little bit more about your organization? How many people, where they are, what their roles are, etc."

Or

Opening: "Thank you for your time today."

Fact Confirmation: "Before we start, I noticed that your company just introduced a new product. Congratulations! How are you doing with it?"

"My intention in the time we have is to understand what are the most important things you wish to achieve, continue, and avoid, and to see if my company can help. Would that be okay?"

OR

Opening: "Thank you for your time today. Oh, I see you are a golfer. Do you get out much? ..."

"My intention in the time we have is to understand what are the most important things you wish to achieve, continue, or avoid, and to see if my company can help. Would that be okay?"

Exercise: Picking up from the last exercise, how would you bring up something that would impress the client or show you have done your homework? Write your answer on a piece of paper.

If you've done your homework, you will be able to put your prospect at ease and learn a few things. That allows you to go on to investigating the next area, priorities.

S.PRI.N.G. DIALOGUES: PRIORITIES

I met with a VP of sales and customer service who told me she wanted to have me train her consultants (people who installed software after it was sold by the sales team) on handling objections. They often received objections that got in the way of a successful implementation and got the company and its customer off on the wrong foot. Instead of diving right in asking her what the objections were, when she wanted to do this training, and what her budget was, I asked her if we could take a step back to understand what might be causing the problems and the environment her people were working in.

We discovered that many of the objections were caused by what salespeople did or didn't say to make a sale, as well as her consultants' lack of involvement in making the sale. I also discovered that her salespeople were not paid commissions on the fees for services so they tended to discount them—but not the software for which they were paid handsomely. The end result is that by taking the time to understand the issues and the client's priorities, I took a half-day day training program and turned it into a three-day program. I increased my sale by 500 percent. Fast forward—because of the good work done for this vice president, I also earned the right to train the salespeople for almost four years, and all because I used the S.PRI.N.G. Dialogue.

True Story

I recently got a call from a person who had been through my training on negotiating. He had just become general manager of a company and wanted me to offer the training in his new company. I said to him, "Before we go any further, would you mind if we took a step back so I can understand the bigger picture and why you want this training?" Long story short, he wanted his people to learn how to increase margins, but our discussion revealed that no matter how much he increased margins via better negotiations, he would never meet his objectives. His biggest priority was driving much more revenue from new and existing customers, as well as shaping the organization in his image. This simple approach turned a nine-thousand-dollar sale into a forty-thousand-dollar sale—and I never made a presentation.

This phase of the S.PRI.N.G. Dialogue focuses on exploring and understanding the priorities prospects have. These priorities are probably the reason they are meeting with you. They want to see if you can help address them. The word *priorities* is meant to be taken broadly; it represents whatever is most important to the people with whom you are speaking. Some examples, depending on with whom you are talking, would be:

- Key projects
- Applications
- Problems
- Goals
- Issues
- Pains
- Key performance indicators
- Competitive issues
- Obstacles
- Areas of focus
- Challenges
- Causes of problems
- Hindrances
- The most important things necessary to reach a goal
- Whatever they are spending their time and energy on.

There are several ways to initiate this phase of the process. A simple but effective way is simply to ask: "May I ask what your three or four most important priorities are?" Or, "May I ask you what your top priorities are for the long and short term?" If you have a lot of experience in a particular industry or working with a certain job title, you might say: "It has been our experience in working with VPs of Sales that three of the top priorities they want to achieve or address are:

1. Selling more to their current prospects.
2. Finding and keeping the best sales personnel.
3. Increasing margins while reducing sales cycles.

Are these your priorities or do you have others?"

I would urge you not to use this approach unless you are truly knowledgeable about a person's responsibilities or a particular industry.

Regardless of how you ask, or what they say, it is imperative for you to explore as best you can each priority with prospects to understand:

- Why it is a priority—and why now. What is the impending or compelling event?
- Who and what is driving the need to do something.
- What is and isn't working.
- What thoughts they have about what is required.
- What is the financial impact of success and failure.
- The impact it has on the individual and the department.
- How does it affects others in the corporation or its customers.
- The company's goals and objectives.
- What they would like to be able to do better or more often to address their priority.
- What the obstacles and challenges to addressing the priority are.
- The dollar amount this priority is costing.
- Who else benefits from this being addressed.
- What are the repercussions of not addressing this (if they say "none," then it really isn't that important).

Below are some examples of a series of questions you can learn to ask for many common priorities a prospect might have or for different types of people or situations:

CFO Questions	1. Where are you spending and where are you cutting back?
	2. What criteria do you use in funding company or departmental initiatives?
	3. What major priorities and initiatives are you funding this year? Where are you cutting back and why?
	4. What are the KPIs (key performance indicators) and why?
	5. What type of business case or return on investment (ROI) do you have to see to invest?
	6. How much autonomy and at what level do people have in spending or allocating their budget?
VP of Sales Questions	1. Tell me about your current sales channels.
	2. How much is direct versus through channels?

(Continued)

	3. What is working and what is not working?
	4. What would you like to do more of?
	5. Where do you need to improve?
	6. What is your current revenue?
	7. What are the plans for next year and the year after?
	8. What role would you like (what you're selling) to play in helping you meet your objectives?
Service and Support Managers	1. Why is this such an important priority?
	2. What is the impact of this on your customers and internally?
	3. What is your company's view of service and where are you falling short?
	4. What service solution do you currently have in place?
	5. What areas do you need to improve?
	6. How is this affecting you financially?
	7. What is your ideal support and service situation like, if anything were possible?
	8. If you could (plant a seed), how would you use that?

"Piece of Cake" Questioning

Using this technique, you will get the most information you can to win business. Why?

- It is easy for you and them.
- Like a round piece of cake, your first question is broad, open ended, and comfortable, which will get them to talk.

Follow that with more specific questions which are intended to:

- Understand the person's priorities.
- Plant seeds for you, your company, and your solution.
- Give you the information you need to win.

Here is an example:

The VP of sales says his/her top priority is more sales. "Piece of Cake" questioning would look like this:

- Tell me more, or, help me understand why this is so important? (Broad and open ended.)
- Why now?
- Who besides yourself feels this is a priority?

- When you say more sales, do you also want to increase margins and profits at the same time, and if so, how much?
- What are you doing to address this?
- What is and isn't working?
- What obstacles would you like to remove and what do you want to be able to do more of?
- What would you like to do that you cannot do at all today?
- What are the major challenges in addressing this?
- What are the financial implications of success or failure around this priority?
- If you haven't already asked, how much do you want to increase your sales by?
- If this happens, what would you be able to do or want to do next?

Planting Seeds

As mentioned earlier, a seed is something about you, your company, your product/offering, or your experience that addresses something the prospect has said. A seed is also a question or series of questions to establish your capabilities or set up your competition. Just like real seeds, they need to be planted deep enough to grow and have an impact on the prospect. You do this by asking them their opinion or thoughts after the seed is planted and whether they would like to see the seed you planted in your proposal and what bearing it will have in their decision. Planting seeds is important because they:

- Influence a person's thinking.
- Establish criteria for your solution and unique aspects of your offer.
- Set traps for the competition.
- Allow you to ask more questions because you are in essence giving the client information about you and your company during the dialogue. Seeds are, in effect, "minipresentations" and prevent you from having to give the "big pitch" and stop you from asking questions.

Here's a true story that shows the value of planting seeds. I sold word processing in the late seventies when it was first becoming popular. This was before PCs and Microsoft Word. At that time, equipment could be as big as a corner credenza and each unit cost around fifteen thousand dollars. The company I worked for, NBI (which stood for Nothing But Initials), handled large complex documents better than anyone. Lawyers, writers, engineers, etc. were prime candidates. Any change to any part of the document reformatted the entire document automatically. The user didn't have to do anything (this system can still do things that today's software can't). One of my larger competitors had a deficiency in managing large documents so they would only show people how changes would occur on a page, but not the whole document because they couldn't do it. Believe it or not, people fell for this because of the name and reputation of the company.

Salespeople in my company learned to ask seed questions that set up the competition and established criteria our competition couldn't address:

- What type of documents do you work with?
- How lengthy are they?
- Do you need to create tables of contents and indexes? If they said "yes," we could do this better than anyone and would explain how.
- Do you often have footnotes? If they said "yes," we would explain how our system handled footnotes automatically.
- How often do you modify them?
- We would plant a seed by telling them to ask and have our competition demonstrate how they handled all the things we did automatically.

If the customer was open and receptive to these ideas and questions, we rarely lost.

Coming back to the example of selling to a VP of sales, planting seeds would look like this:

The VP of sales says their top priority is more sales.

- Tell me more or help me understand why this is so important (broad and open ended).
- Why now?
- When you say more sales, do you also want to increase margins and profits at the same time?
- Why is this happening?
- What are you doing to address this?
- What is and isn't working?
- What obstacles would you like to remove and what do you want to be able to do more of?
- **Seed:** Our program has a feature called "Obstacle Buster," which teaches your people how to anticipate these obstacles so people can be more successful. How does that sound to you?
- What would you like to do that you cannot do at all today?
- **Seed:** If you could integrate all the key teaching points into your Customer Relationship Managements (CRM) so it is simple and easy to use and track, would that be something you would want to see in your solution?
- **Seed:** We have a client that had a similar problem and we [tell them a short story of what you did]. How would that work for you? Would you want to see that in your solution?
- What are the financial implications of success or failure around this priority?
- How much do you want to increase your sales by?
- If this happens, what would you be able to do or want to do next?

Exercise: On Table 6.1 write down your most unique offerings or things you do better than your competition. Then translate them into questions you might ask or anecdotes you might tell.

Table 6.1
Planting Seeds for Your Unique Offerings

Unique offering or what you do better than others	Questions you would ask Anecdote you might tell

S.PRI.N.G. DIALOGUES: NEEDS

This phase of the initial meeting focuses on two key components:

- Further exploration of what they need to do to solve and address their priorities. This is also an excellent time to plant more seeds.
- What you need to know to win the business.

The reason we suggest you ask these questions during this phase is that people are usually reluctant to answer them earlier in the dialogue. As mentioned in the opening of this chapter, prospects generally don't trust salespeople and feel like they lose their leverage or power by telling you certain things. If you have done what has been suggested, people will be more open to answering you because they are already thinking they want to buy from you and you have "earned the right" by handling yourself more professionally and differently.

Please note that no technique works all the time, so you won't always get the answers you want every time you ask. In fact, you may need to ask them in separate meetings or have someone else ask them later in the sales process (a person who isn't a salesperson is always more trusted and would be a good person to ask).

Use this time to ask all the questions for which you must have answers to win a deal. This is also an excellent time to plant more seeds and establish criteria by asking hypothetical questions such as "wouldn't it be nice," "what if," or "just suppose." This will reveal capabilities they want that the competition doesn't have, but you do. It will also help you develop your presentation or demonstration that is key to winning business.

On the following pages you will find a number of key questions to ask during this phase of the interaction. You may not be able to ask all of these in one meeting, but it is important to know the answers to these if you want to win more opportunities.

Hypothetical Questions—Open People's Minds to What They Don't Have and How You Can Help
If we could do anything for you that you can't do today, what would that be?
What are the top items on your wish list that you cannot currently do today?
If you could [mention something unique] how would you use it?
YOU TRY ONE

The second part of the Needs section is to get the information you need to qualify, present, and win. Below are many ways to ask with space for you to practice.

Questions about the Decision Process
What are the steps involved in issuing a purchase order? Who gets involved at each step and what role do they play?
In the past, how have you made decisions of this nature?
Besides yourself, who else is involved in this decision? What role do they play?
Can you diagram for me the steps involved and who gets involved at each step? What is their role?

YOU TRY ONE

Questions about When a Decision Is Going to Be Made
When will you make a decision?
When do you want to be able to use or launch the products or systems you are buying?
Why then?
What happens if you miss those dates? What are the repercussions?
What if anything could prevent this from happening?

YOU TRY ONE

(*Continued*)

Questions about How Important Doing Something Is
Of all the things you need to do, where does this rank?
On a scale of 1 to 10 with 10 being most important, where would you
  rank this and why?
Where on your radar is doing something to address these priorities?
What if anything could prevent this from happening?

YOU TRY ONE

Questions about Who You Are Competing With
What other alternatives are you considering?
Who else, if anybody, are you looking at?
How else might you address this?
If you are looking at others, who, and why did you choose them?
Did anyone in the decision process bring them in or have a preference?
Is there anything you have seen or heard that you would want to make
  sure we can do as well, or better?
What haven't you heard that you wish you had?

YOU TRY ONE

Questions about Decision Criteria
What criteria will you use to make your decision?
Why are those the criteria you settled on? Who else was involved?
Can you rank those for me?
Earlier I mentioned a few things [seeds] that you seemed to like. How
  would those get built into your formal criteria?

YOU TRY ONE

Questions about Obstacles
How could this decision be deferred or stopped?
What obstacles do you see internally or externally that could prevent
  this from happening?
What would be the consequences of that?
What can be done to anticipate these so they won't happen?
Who could prevent this from happening?

YOU TRY ONE

Questions about the Decision Maker
Who ultimately decides?
Who has final signature authority for this?
Who could prevent this from happening?

YOU TRY ONE

Questions about Money and Budget
Have you budgeted for this?
What variables or factors did you use to create your budget?
How much did you budget?
What have you done in the past to fund projects that aren't budgeted? Will you do so this time?
Are you competing for budget dollars or is there a specific line item for this?
Whose money is it?
Does anyone have to approve the expenditure besides yourself?
Based upon the info I have now, your investment would be around (give them an estimate). Would that work or is it too low/high?
We have three solutions at three different price ranges. The first is X$, the second is Y$, and the third is Z$. Which is most appropriate?
If you are not comfortable telling me your budget, can you give me a range? I ask because I don't want to underbuild or overbuild your solution.
If someone (including me) comes in with the perfect solution but it is more expensive, how will you handle that? What have you done in the past?

YOU TRY ONE

S.PRI.N.G. DIALOGUES: GAINS

Winning the sale is easier if you know what is at stake for the prospect, professionally and personally. People buy something if it helps them get what they want and/or avoid what they don't want. In other words, all salespeople and their solutions are a means to an end. People want what you're selling because it will help them in some way.

The more personal and more immediate, the more likely people will buy something.

Table 6.2 shows some things people want to avoid, or want to attain by buying something.

It is important to ask the prospects about their needs so that they can envision them and, more important, associate them with you and your offer.

Table 6.2
Things People Want or Want to Avoid

WANT	AVOID	PROFESSIONAL OR PERSONAL
Make more money	Being passed over for a promotion	Personal
Job security	Being woken up at 3AM with business problems	Professional
Be home with family	Long hours	Personal
Get promoted	Getting fired	Professional
Add a skill to their resume	Being stuck in old technology or job	Professional

Here are some ways to ask:

- "What would it mean to you professionally if these priorities were met?"
- "What would it mean for you personally?"
- "Imagine you are getting your review next year and these priorities were all addressed. What would things look like? What would happen in your review?"
- "If you could successfully address [repeat their priorities], what would that mean to you?"

To any of the above, you can add:

- "And what if you don't address these priorities? What would that mean and what do things look like then?"

Exercise: Write a question to find out their gain and what it would mean if it were to happen. How would you ask it in a way that introduces some fear?

After the S.PRI.N.G. Dialogue

It is possible that after the dialogue your prospect will want some form of presentation. If you have to, use what you learned in your S.PRI.N.G. Dialogue to tailor your presentation to what you heard. Unless you are selling something that can be sold on the first call, keep it brief and set up a next meeting. If you have planted seeds properly, you may not have to do any presentation until the next time you meet, or if you do, it won't have to be as lengthy because you already told them a lot via the seeds.

Next Steps: After your S.PRI.N.G. Dialogue (or after your brief presentation), you must recommend next steps. This shows commitment on the prospect's part and puts you in control of the sales process. Try and get commitment to next steps that favor you over the competition, including:

- Visiting your prospects.
- your prospects coming to your office or headquarters.
- your prospects meeting with your executives.
- Having another meeting for more details before you give them a proposal.
- Setting up a second meeting.

In your world, what might be some next steps you would recommend?

If possible, you should also try and have them do some things for you, which gets them to commit to you during the sales cycle. Some examples of this include:

- Getting you some information.
- Introducing you to other people involved in the decision.
- Responding to your e-mails.
- Having a meal with you.

Use Table 6.3 to prepare for a call or to examine if you got the information you needed after your first meeting.

Table 6.3
S.PRI.N.G. Dialogue Checklist

Item	Comments
Are you talking to the right person? Is it the decision maker (DM)?	
Do you know their DiSC style and how will you adjust?	
How will you create rapport in the beginning?	
Do you know their current situation?	
What business priorities and/or problems of the individual, the project, and/or the company are you solving for them? IS THERE AN IMPENDING EVENT?	

(Continued)

Table 6.3 (*Continued*)
S.PRI.N.G. Dialogue Checklist

Item	Comments
Do you have any idea of the financial implications of addressing these priorities for the client?	
What seeds and criteria will you plant for your company? How will you differentiate yourselves?	
How will you ask about the competition?	
How will you ask about the buying criteria?	
How will you ask about the decision process?	
How will you ask about timing?	
How will you ask about budget?	
How will you ask about their gain?	
If we don't know the DM, what are we doing to find out and meet with DM?	
How well did you take control of the sales cycle and create next steps to keep the opportunity on track?	

R.E.A.L. TIPS AND REMINDERS

☑ Confirm the amount of time in the Situation phase to judge how much time you can spend in each segment of the dialogue.

☑ Ask about or confirm some of the things you have researched (not too many, or it will be boring or sound like an interrogation).

☑ Add the ice breaker (something you saw on their website about the company or them, an industry event, an observation about something in their office, hometown, etc.) either before or after your opening.

☑ Even though you are using the structure of a S.PRI.N.G. Dialogue, keep it conversational.

☑ Always prepare by having questions you want to ask written down. Don't be afraid to look at them as a reference.

☑ Prepare so you feel confident without being arrogant.

☑ Practice makes perfect. Role-play with someone before you go on the call.

☑ Practice in "team meetings."

☑ Adjust to the person's DiSC style so they are comfortable with you. If they are a High S or I, take a bit longer in the S part of the dialogue to create a good environment.

☑ Remember the word *priorities* is meant to embrace many other meanings including projects, goals, issues, challenges, initiatives, etc.

☑ If someone says she has only one priority, ask her what the most important thing is she must do to address the priority.

☑ Know what differentiates you so you can plant seeds.

☑ Remind people of the seeds they reacted to when asking them about their criteria to see if they will include those.

☑ Take notes. There is no way you can remember everything without doing so.

- Write down questions you could ask for any priority a prospect might have.
- Think of the priorities, concerns, problems, and goals that you often hear. Write down any additional questions you could ask about a specific priority.
- If you work with others, take some time to brainstorm and role-play with them.

☑ Use the S.PRI.N.G. Dialogue outlined in this book.

☑ Create a S.PRI.N.G. Dialogue form for yourself.

7

Presenting or Demonstrating Your Solution

Anytime you suggest something to a prospect, you are making a type of a presentation. Just like a present, they come in all shapes and sizes, from sitting across a table sharing a cup of coffee (or tea and crumpets) to presenting to one hundred people in an auditorium. In all instances, there are common attributes and skills needed to be a great presenter that we discuss in this chapter.

PRESENTATIONS

If you do the things outlined in previous chapters, any presentation or demonstration will have an even greater impact. These include whether you are in your "Sweet Spot," are speaking to the right person/s, have qualified the opportunity properly, have built good rapport and credibility, have done a good S.PRI.N.G. Dialogue (including planting deep seeds), and have established your expertise. If you have not done these things, your presentation or demonstration will not be nearly as effective, and your chances of winning business will be severely minimized. (Of course, you can just drop your price, but that is a very dangerous habit to get into.)

Elements that go into making an effective presentation or demonstration, and how well it is received, include:

1. The structure of your presentation.
2. The environment you are presenting in (in person, over the phone, via the web, over lunch, etc.).
3. How many people to whom you are presenting.
4. Adjustments for the DiSC style/s of the audience.
5. If in a competitive situation, setting traps for the competition and differentiating yourself.
6. How much and well you engage and/or capture your audience's attention.
7. The level of trust and comfort between you and the audience.
8. How many people from your company are involved in the presentation.

9. How much you have practiced beforehand (no matter how many times you have done it).
10. How interested the prospect is in you and your offering.
11. How skilled, enthusiastic, and passionate you are about what you are presenting.
12. How well you have delineated the benefits of your offering throughout the presentation or demonstration.

This chapter takes you through many of these elements so your presentations and/or demonstrations have more impact and help you win more business.

The Structure of Your Presentation or Demonstration

A presentation/demonstration delivered in any format or environment should basically have the structure or flow described below (please note the order can sometimes change but should contain these elements):

How Do You Start? Does It Get Their Attention?

My wife and I had just moved from Washington, D.C., to New Jersey and we were in need of a vacuum cleaner. We called the Electrolux representative to come meet with us. After initial greetings, he took out a bag of dirt and dust and threw it on our floor. Needless to say it got our attention and set the stage for the rest of his demonstration in which he showed us how he picked up all the dirt he had laid down and more. We bought the vacuum cleaner even though it was very expensive. It lasted for more than twenty years.

I will often start with a dollar amount benefit that my work will achieve for them to get their attention. Another attention getter is a "before" and "after" image of the impact of my training. Other good ways to start are to show pictures of the positive impact your solution has, play a video, provide testimonials, or show a sense of humor in some way. The tools available to you via your PC or Mac allow you to do almost anything you want. It all depends on how creative you are.

Introduce Your People First in an Illustrative Way

This step assumes you have other people in your organization to help you present. A common mistake salespeople make is trying to make presentations themselves when other people delivering the same information will have much greater impact. For example, a technical person has much more credibility than a salesperson when describing the internal workings of a system. When you introduce one of your team members, take care to emphasize accomplishments. Before giving a speech, someone usually introduces the guest speakers and lists their credentials. This is done so the audience will be more appreciative, respectful, and more receptive to the speaker. The same should be done in business. All too often, a salesperson will present other people involved simply by their title, which does nothing for them or the audience. Here is an example: If someone were to present the writer of this book (Jonathan London) by saying "Our next speaker is Jonathan London. He has written the book *The Entrepreneur's Guide to Selling*." End of introduction.

Compare that introduction to this one: "Our next speaker is Jonathan London. He has written the book *The Entrepreneur's Guide to Selling*. Prior to writing this book, Jonathan had been the top salesperson or manager in the world for all the different companies he worked for. He has had extensive training and has also trained approximately fourteen thousand people in twenty-three countries. Some of his customers include...." The latter sounds more impressive. This is what you should do when you present the people on your team. Let prospects know their credentials and background so when your team members speak, prospects listen. If you are the only person, it is OK to introduce your credentials but try to do so in a humble way.

Have the Prospects Introduce Their People with Role/Title

Quite often you will meet people for the first time at a presentation. These people are there for a reason and play a role in the decision. In fact, one or more will often be the decision maker, so it is critical to know who they are, what their role or title is, and what they would like to see or get from the time spent (which you can do here or in Step 4). One last note: These people are often High D's and i's (in the DiSC system) so you need to engage them early—something this step does.

Give an Overview of the Agenda Including Time Frames

There is an old expression in sales: "Tell them what you are going to tell them, tell them, and then tell them what you told them." This step is telling them what you are going to tell them. Please note you should confirm that the agenda and time frames work for the audience. An example would be:

- Introductions
- Current situation and confirmation of the prospect's priorities and needs (a.k.a. executive summary)
- Your company's background
- Your solution to address their priorities and criteria
- References
- Investment page
- Next steps

Some people like to introduce the agenda before introducing their people. Both are fine.

Review and Confirm Understanding of Current Situation—
See if There Are Any Changes

Sometimes referred to as "The Executive Overview," this should be a reiteration of what you have discovered in your S.PRI.N.G. Dialogues. If you have interviewed several people, you should prioritize the items by the importance of the people you are presenting to. For example, if you interviewed the decision maker and two other people with whom the decision maker asked you to speak, you would list the priorities, needs, and concerns of the decision maker first.

The overview should also include challenges and desired changes to address their priorities and concerns.

The reasons you should do this review are:

- To let the person/people know you have heard and understand their plight.
- To see if there have been any changes.
- To give people you have not met (especially if it is the decision maker) a chance to air their thoughts.

Ask if anything has changed, taken higher priority, or needs to be added. If anything has changed, put those changes on a flip chart or board so you don't forget to address them.

Present Your Corporate or Company Pitch

A company's background quite often determines the products and services it will offer. Its history can be a great indicator to what will come and how a company handles different situations. For example, when people buy a Mercedes Benz or BMW, they are also buying the company's background and legacy of making powerful, well-engineered cars. On the other hand, when Volkswagen introduced the Phaeton, a car to compete with Mercedes and BMW, it failed miserably, even though the reviews of it were exceptional. Why? Primarily because people couldn't see VW making that kind of car, and if they were spending a lot of money they wanted the prestige of the BMW or Mercedes label. (Lesson: Stay in your Sweet Spot.) Even if you have delivered your corporate presentation once before, you want to do it again (perhaps a bit shorter) for several reasons:

- It may have been awhile since you last did so.
- There might be new people you are presenting to who have not seen it.
- People forget things or get confused as to which vendor said what.

Make sure that you describe the benefits of your company to the prospect. Many people give a lot of facts about their company but don't relate the benefit. For example, a company I work with has been in its industry for eight years, has sixteen thousand customers, and more than twenty-five hundred employees. This is worth touting—such a solid company is a benefit in and of itself. But some presenters gloss over it because they have said it so many times. This is a big mistake. The benefits must be expressed. We talk about this much more later in the chapter.

Present or Demonstrate Your Solution

A solution is a compilation and/or integration of standard capabilities (software, hardware, services, etc.) that looks unique to the prospect because of how you put them together. It is based on what you discovered and the seeds you planted in the S.PRI.N.G. Dialogue as well as the criteria customers will use to make their decision. Choose the top capabilities that are most unique to you and most relevant to the S.PRI.N.G. Dialogue.

Recently, my wife needed a new bike. She wanted something more similar to what she grew up with in Germany than what is normally in bike shops in our neighborhood. The salesperson at the bike store asked us what she wanted and she told him higher handlebars, fenders, a basket in front, a certain color, etc. He told us he would get back to us the next day, which he did and told her he could give her what she wanted. His solution was putting together a bike that was exactly what my wife wanted by putting standard parts together. As part of his solution, he also offered us an extended service package, which truly made his offer unique because other stores in the neighborhood don't do that.

While selling videoconferencing, we had an 80 percent close rate when we customized our presentations and demonstrations based on what the prospect's priorities and needs were. Unfortunately, we only customized 20 percent because we were not organized enough to do it more often.

Do you know your products and services well enough to put together unique solutions? If not, you should, especially if you have a limited offer and have to do more with less. You must be able to relate how your offer would address a prospect's priorities and needs in a way that is better than other alternatives. One way of doing this is by turning a deficit into a feature. Let me give you an example. Going back to the days I was selling word processing, competitors like Wang, DEC, Lanier, and IBM all offered products with their own hardware and software. Two of these (the bigger companies) had a weak offering with limited functionality in key areas. They could get away with limited functionality because of their name and reputation, but this limitation was a problem for many of their customers. Their solution was to actually make a "feature" out of this limitation by describing it as a "customization feature" that allowed customers to program the system their own way. They said that the "customization feature" gave the end user even greater capability than the systems that had more functionality as a standard part of their offering. The only problem was you had to be Einstein to figure it out, and if Einstein was sick or left the company, there was trouble.

A simpler example might be recent offerings of camcorders that have fewer features. The benefit of this is they are easier to use (thus used more), have fewer parts to break, are easier to carry around (which again gets more use), and are less expensive. These benefits have to be sold and presented to outweigh the features they do not have.

Show Your ROI, TCO, TTV, and Other Nonfinancial Benefits

Showing cold, hard figures that delineate the financial benefits of your solution can be very persuasive. But ROI (return on investment), TCO (total cost of ownership), and TTV (time to value) can be very scary and complicated subjects. If you are selling to a CFO or someone with a strong financial background, their standards, measurements, and language/terminology around ROI, TCO, and TTV can be like a foreign language to salespeople. That is why I like to keep it simple by putting financial benefits into three categories:

- How much it can save the prospect (often known as hard dollar savings).
- How much it allows the prospect to defer or avoid spending (which sometimes looks like saving).
- How much the prospect can make from the offer (often the biggest number but known as "soft").

Let's go back to the bicycle example. Let's say it cost us five hundred dollars to buy the bicycle, two hundred dollars more than another bike we are looking at. How much can I save or defer spending with this bike? At the moment, the bike isn't associated with any profits because my wife will be riding for pleasure (and doesn't want to have a newspaper route, which I still don't understand). But we can still calculate a savings as shown in Table 7.1.

So how do you calculate the ROI? One way is calculate the savings/deferred total in comparison to the price difference of the other bike. So, because the total savings is $403.00 and the other bike was $200, your ROI is approximately half a year ($200/$403 = .496). If you want to get really fancy, you can extend the financial benefit over the second year and add another $403.00 of benefit. You can also compare both years' savings to the purchase price so the real price of the bike is $500 − $806 = actual savings of $306. The bike didn't cost anything. This calculation can also be considered the TCO because it delineates what expenses are involved in owning this bike for two years.

TCO takes on more considerations, including the cost of people and goods to take care of something you are selling. BMW has done a tremendous job with this by offering a four-year lease that has zero cost of ownership because it takes care of everything for the four years you lease their car. When you compare that with buying a car, changing the oil, tires, wipers, and anything out of warranty after the warranty period, BMW's offer is very appealing, plus it is a great car.

Table 7.1
Sample ROI on Bike Costing $500

Feature	Save	Defer/Avoid
Puncture-Proof Tires	Bike more—save gas—1 gallon a month @ $2.50/gallon = $30.00	Better tires need to be replaced less often— $24/year with service.
Basket	Use for shopping—add an additional gallon/ month = $2.50 × 12 = $30	Excess wear and tear on my car. Less repairs— less oil change. Avoid one oil change a year— $50 (I live in NYC).
Bigger Seat	My wife happens to have a bad back so this is critical. She has been to a chiropractor many times. Saves one trip = $90.	It is also safer so there is less chance of a mishap (going into a pot hole or skidding on gravel, etc.).
2 Years Free Service	The other shops only offered 1 year. A spring cleaning is $79.	Avoid 2nd year of ser- vice by other stores— 2nd year is $100.
1 Yr. Sub-Total	$229.00	$174.00
TOTAL SAVINGS	(Save and Defer)	$403.00

Making Money: Let's say I can convince my wife that she should use her bike to make some money and we agree it will be to sell her delicious home-baked cookies (eat 'em and weep Mrs. Fields), not have a newspaper route. They sell for $8.00 a dozen, and she thinks she can sell twelve dozen a month if she makes them by hand. That is $96 a month or $1,152.00 a year. Amazingly enough, the bike has an attachment to the back wheel ($89) that helps her make the dough for the cookies twice as fast when she peddles on a stationary stand (which cost her $79) versus by hand. Now she can sell an additional dozen a month, which is $96.00 more per month, for an additional annual earnings of $1,152. Let's take a look at her ROI now in Table 7.2.

Nonfinancial Benefits: These can often be more compelling and emo- tional than the financial. For my wife, they are:

- A feeling of safety
- A desire to ride more
- Being in better physical condition and health—staving off getting older
- Less back pain

Table 7.2
Sample ROI on Bike Costing $668.00 (includes stationary stand and attachment to make dough)

Feature	Save	Defer/Avoid	Make Money
Puncture Proof Tires	Bike more—save gas—1 gallon a month = $30.00	Less expensive tires need to be replaced more often—$24/year with service.	
Basket	Use for shopping—add an additional gallon/month = $2.50 × 12 = $30	Excess wear and tear on my car. Less repairs—less oil change. Avoid one oil change a year—$50	
Bigger Seat	My wife happens to have a bad back so this is critical. She has been to a chiropractor many times. Save one trip = $90	It is also safer so there is less chance of a mishap (going into a pot hole or skidding on gravel, etc.).	
Bike Stand	n/a	n/a	n/a
Attachment to Make Dough Twice as Fast	n/a	n/a	$96 a month or $1,152.00 for the year.
2 Years Free Service	The other shops only offered 1 year. A Spring cleaning is $79.	Avoid 2nd year of service by other stores—2nd year is $100	
TOTAL 1 YEAR ROI (Save, Make, and Defer)	$229.00 (save)	$174.00 (defer)	$1,152.00 (make)
$1,555.00 for a $668.00 bike, which is a 233% ROI: ($1,555/$668)			$1,555.00

- A return to her youth by having a bike that is similar to when she was a child
- Having more money to do what she wants versus worrying about our money and what she should or shouldn't spend

Provide References

References are independent proof from someone who has previously purchased your product or service, or an impartial recommender (a magazine or organization that does reviews in an industry, like *Car and Driver* magazine or *Consumer Reports*). They are important because more than ever people buy today based on peer or independent recommendations. This has always been important but with the Internet, even more so. For example, TripAdvisor is a huge success because it is an independent way for people to get information that is not from a salesperson.

Being proactive with references gives a prospect confidence that you are being up front and honest. In most cases, the prospects won't even call the references because they know they will be glowing, but not doing it might be interpreted as not having any, which could really hurt your sale. If you are selling a brand-new product or service, a good idea is to give your product to some people or companies at a nominal fee, or even for free so they can become your reference.

Provide Summary, Take Questions and Give Answers, and Define Next Steps (including Trial Close if Appropriate)

You have already told them what you were going to tell them, and then you told them. Now you have to tell them what you told them by summarizing your presentation or demonstration. Some ways of doing this are:

- Provide a handout of the five key points you want them to remember.
- Ask them what they were most impressed with and any concerns they have (you then know where they stand more completely, and if you have time, you can handle the concerns right there). If they have few or no concerns, you should definitely trial close them. This means ask for the sale.
- A lot of salespeople will end a presentation or demonstration with no specific actions to be taken. At a minimum, there is a specific day and time to discuss their reaction to your presentation or next steps to move forward.

Tailor the Presentation to the Environment

The environment in which you make the presentation is critical. Additionally, which media or technology you use will be important. Each has its own unique properties.

One example of environment is when you are dining or going for a cup of coffee. These presentations would be mostly verbal with notes or even scribbling on a pad. Do so after the meal, making sure you leave yourself enough time. Some samples to show are good to have as well. Have a notepad to draw diagrams and take notes.

Another choice is a one-on-one meeting in an office. With this choice, you can have a proposal that you review or use a whiteboard or flip chart to illustrate key points. You can also use PowerPoint, presentation samples, or a written proposal. Furthermore, you can present via video or web conferencing, or over the phone.

It is always best to present in person if you can manage to do so. Next best would be through high-quality videoconferencing. After that, web conferencing is great because it is inexpensive and allows you to present as if you were in person. Make sure your phone or speakerphone is high quality and well positioned. "Trial close" more often with the client when there is no visual aspect to the presentation to make sure things are going well and you are on the right track. For example:

- How does this sound to you?
- What are your thoughts about what I just presented?
- Do you have any concerns or questions?

For group presentations, use:

- PowerPoint
- Whiteboard
- Flip charts
- Presentation samples
- Written proposal
- Video or web conferencing
- Conference call over a speakerphone.

You should try to avoid presenting over the phone to a large group.

The structure of your presentation should be pretty much the same in any environment. The main difference will be how much media or technology you can use versus just talking about things and the amount of time you might give each. Table 7.3 reiterates and provides some additional clarity.

Adjust Your Presentations for Different DiSC Styles

Table 7.4 shows how to adjust your presentations when presenting to the different DiSC ® styles.

When presenting to a group, you should always present with an eye to the priorities of the decision maker first. However, you should also present in order of impatience. This can be confusing so let's go back to the bicycle story. When we were buying her bike, the salesperson recognized I was a "High Di" DiSC style because I was enthusiastic, asking him about all kinds of features, not letting him finish, telling my wife how great that was, etc. My wife on the other hand was patient, didn't interrupt, and waited for

Table 7.3
Presentation Environment Options

Environment	Media or Technology	Comments
Dining, Cup of Coffee, 1:1	• Mostly verbal with notes • Use a whiteboard or flip chart to illustrate key points.	• Present after the meal and make sure you leave yourself enough time. • Some samples to show are good to have as well. • Have a notepad to draw diagrams and take notes.
1:1 Meeting	• Powerpoints • Whiteboard • Flip charts • Presentation samples • Written proposal • Video or Web conferencing • Discuss verbally • Discuss over phone	• All of these can work well. • It is always best to be in person if you can manage to do so. • Next best would be over video conferencing if it is high quality. • Web conferencing is next best since it allows you to present as if you were in person over the web. • Make sure phone or speakerphone is high quality and well positioned. • "Trial close" more often with the client when there is no visual to make sure things are going well and you are on the right track.
Group Meeting	• Powerpoints • Whiteboard • Flip charts • Presentation Samples • Written proposal • Video or Web conferencing • Discuss over speakerphone	• You should try to avoid presenting over the phone to a group. • At a minimum, try to have a visual if you cannot be physically there. This is why Web conferencing is important. • Make sure phone or speakerphone is high quality and well positioned with group. • "Trial close" more often with the client when there is no visual to make sure things are going well and you are on the right track.

Table 7.4
Adjusting Your Presentation to Different DiSC® Styles

DiSC® Style	Pace	Your Tone of Voice	Presenting Tips
Dominant	Fast	Confident, strong, but supportive of the prospect	Don't waste too much time up front—get right into the presentation. Less is more. Use bullet points. Be direct and to the point—focus on control and results.
Influential	Fast	Expressive, outgoing, animated	Start out in a very friendly way. Spend a few minutes talking before you start—be more positive and effusive—paint a big picture of the possibilities. Use more stories, pictures, and analogies. Avoid being impatient when they ramble.
Steadfast	Slower	Calm, easy, comfortable, supportive	Start out in a very friendly way—spend a few minutes talking before you start. Be very orderly, explain how things work, finish one thing before you go on with another. Get their feedback if they are quiet to make sure you are on track. Don't propose too many things or brand-new things. If you ask a question, don't interrupt and let them answer.
Conscientious	Slower	Analytical, less emotional, logical	Don't waste too much time up front—get right into the presentation/demonstration. Have lots of information to support your statements. Focus on quality and accuracy. The more independent and unbiased the better. Don't be bothered by their cynicism or lack of reaction. If you ask a question, don't interrupt and let them answer. They need to think about things.

the whole explanation (which is why we get into arguments, but that is a whole other story). When he started to present the most important features of his offer, he would say something like, "The bike comes with a year warranty and is nearly indestructible." (I felt like Superman.) He would then explain why, by going into minute detail about the carbon/aluminum/resin blah blah blah construction which I had stopped listening to, but my wife not only listened to, but asked questions about.

So, if with a group:

- Present at a high level as if you were presenting only to High D's and i's.
- Then present all the process and detail to the High S's and C's. They are much more patient listeners.

You can do this point by point, or do an executive summary of all the key points and then come back to each one in detail (which is my preference because I don't want the D's and i's fading out).

Set Traps for the Competition and Differentiate Yourself

A trap is something that anticipates what the competition is going to say or do and catches them when they do it. The best example I can give is when we were selling NBI Word Processing. We knew how our competitors would demonstrate their equipment to hide certain deficiencies. So we would demo ours and tell them to have the competitor show them exactly the same thing without skipping steps. It worked every time, until they realized we were on to them and changed their demo so we had to relearn what they did and set new traps.

You can set traps as explicitly as just described, or more subtly by saying things like, "We don't believe anyone else can do this," or "We have been told we are unique in this capability," and have the prospect verify it for themselves. You can also have someone else set the trap, for instance a non-salesperson or someone at the prospect's company who wants you to win and will set the traps for you. Any trap, set by anyone, can also be a subtle, casual remark like "I overheard," or "I am not sure but I think," "Someone told me," or "I overheard someone say," etc.

Since my earliest days of selling I have created "good faith comparison tables" prospects can use that compare the capabilities of my capabilities versus competitors. I call it good faith so they know it is based on the latest information I have and could have changed so I don't set a trap for myself. You should always be honest, tell the truth, and never lie. It builds your credibility tremendously, even more so if they catch the competition lying. An example can be found in Table 7.5.

Orchestrate Team Presentations

A good salesperson is as much an orchestrator as a presenter when others are available to help. Assuming you have competent people, you

Table 7.5
Good Faith Comparison Table: Sample of IPG against XYZ

Item	IPG	XYZ	Comments
Develop effective strategies	Yes	Yes	This is the culmination of activities and skills addressed in IPG's program. Both organizations address the appropriate strategy. IPG also provides the tactics and skills to implement the strategy.
Online tools	Yes	?	IPG's implementation drives usage and results.
Paperlite tools use after class	Yes	?	If has to be easy or people wont use it.
Facilitated by senior executives	Yes	Yes	Critical for credibility and acceptance of materials by people attending class.
Identify Ideal Prospect	Yes	Yes	Both companies do well.
Tools to prospect to end users	Yes	?	Must happen to develop effective account or opportunity strategies.
Adapt to different DiSC styles	Yes	No	People buy from people they are comfortable with and trust. This element of selling is essential at all phases of the sales cycle.

should let them be the SMEs (subject matter experts) at the appropriate time in your presentation. Technical people should present the technical elements, support people your service programs, etc. Always coordinate and practice the presentation beforehand so everyone knows their role and when to answer a question or not. This is especially important if a prospect is visiting your headquarters and is meeting people who don't report to you. When I worked for NBI and PictureTel, the salespeople were required to fill out a document detailing for all presenters what their role was, the competition, the people attending, and more, so they had as much impact as possible. In addition, the salesperson had to be at HQ one day before to practice. We had a very high close rate doing this. Whenever you have a big opportunity, you should plan accordingly.

Get the Prospect Involved

There are many ways to get people involved in your presentation. The simplest is just asking the prospects questions or getting their thoughts and feelings about your presentation or demonstration. Trial closes (discussed in Chapter 11) get people involved. Doing some fun quizzing or Q + A during a presentation is also a good way to get people involved. You can do this as your creative beginning or your summary of your presentation.

If you are doing some kind of demo, having people try your product is the best way. Even better, if you can and the product allows it, let them use the product for a period of time so they get used to it, comfortable with it, and don't want to give it back. A conditional purchase or "buy and try" allows people to try it knowing they get all or most of their money back if they don't want it.

Understand: Structure and Knowledge Are Nothing without Passion

A prospect will only get as excited about your product or offering as you are. Passion and emotion are contagious and you need to imbue your presentation with as much as possible. I am not talking about the people on the infomercials who come across as phony. I am talking about a confidence (not arrogance), something grounded, sincere, and real. To this day, the greatest speaker I have ever seen or heard was Martin Luther King. I still get emotional when I hear him speak. He was a tremendous orator who brought together passion, knowledge, focus, commitment, a wonderful vocabulary, and more. He captured his audience with his intensity and his ability to relate his message to the millions of people who listened to him. Great salespeople need to embody all of these elements when they present. Obviously, selling something is usually less profound or relevant than the social issues Dr. King was discussing, but the way he spoke is just as important in making a presentation.

You should think about when you were moved by a presentation. What was it that did so? How important was the subject to you? What qualities did the presenter exhibit—intelligence, sense of humor, caring? Find the ones that you think are most important to you, those you feel least confident in, and practice them.

Employ Stories, Anecdotes, and Analogies

The best way to get a point across is to use one of these three approaches. They all capture people's imagination, give context to the data so they can understand it better, and break down some of the boundaries between you and the prospect. Wikipedia defines *storytelling* as "the art of portraying real or fictitious events in words, images, and sounds. Stories are told for entertainment purposes, and often to teach lessons and provide morals." I have been using stories throughout this book to illustrate key points, and I hope you have enjoyed them. I do the same when I am selling or in a training class. I am told these are the favorite part for the audience.

Wikipedia defines an *anecdote* this way: "A brief tale narrating an interesting or amusing biographical incident.... An anecdote is always based on real life, an incident involving actual persons, whether famous or not, in real places."

An example of an anecdote would be telling a prospect about a customer who had a similar situation and how you approached or resolved it.

Finally, Dictionary.com (why give Wikipedia all the fun?) defines an *analogy* as: "1. a similarity between like features of two things, on which a comparison may be based: *the analogy between the heart and a pump.* 2. similarity or comparability."

An example of an analogy would be comparing your product or service, which might be more expensive than your competition's, to the prospect's product or service—that is more expensive than its competitors' offerings. (There is a great story about this in Chapter 8.)

If you don't know already, spend some time researching the best stories, analogies, and anecdotes you can use in your presentations and demonstrations. Your personal history and sales experience should offer you many.

Express Benefits

Too many salespeople make the mistake of describing something and assume the prospect will understand the benefits. Regardless of the format, environment, or situation, you must tell people the benefits of your offering. This increases the chances of a prospect taking an action up to 73 percent. Why? Because benefits are the only thing that matters to the prospect. Everything else is just a description of something. A simple and effective way of doing this is following the Feature-Function-Benefit model as shown in Table 7.6.

GENERAL PRESENTATION TIPS

Practice makes perfect: Presentations go better when you prepare beforehand and tailor the presentation to the customer/prospect's particular requirements. Practice your presentation in front of a video camera or tape recorder to see and hear how you sound. Feeling nervous before you present is normal. (Bill Russell, the great Boston Celtics center, would throw up before every game.) Advance preparation and practice will help you control your nervousness.

Try to gain access to the presentation room early. Get a "feel" for the room first. Put yourself in the audience seats and "check the angles." Make sure your laptop/projector works, is set optimally on the screen, and "set your marks" so that you don't block the screen.

Wear something that gives you confidence. Dress appropriately for the audience to whom you are presenting. For example, don't wear a suit when presenting to coal miners.

Plan your presentation: See the presentation planner in the Appendix. Know your prospect's priorities, needs, and what they hope to gain and want to avoid from occurring. Any idea or suggestion is a

Table 7.6
Feature-Function-Benefit for a Sales Training Offer Using an iPod

PROSPECT'S PRIORITY	FEATURE/ FUNCTION PRODUCT/ OFFERING	OPERATIONAL/TECHNI- CAL/FUNCTIONAL BENEFIT	BUSINESS/FINANCIAL DEPARTMENT BENEFIT	INDIVIDUAL OR COMPANY BENEFIT
Improve sales productivity	Record lessons on iPod	• Easy to use • Can listen while in car or over lunch • Can listen when needed for better retention	• Approximately $150 less per student × 100 students • Close one more sale per person of $500/person • Total of $65,000	• Increased earnings and reduced costs can be used to fund additional technology • VP of Sales gets promoted to EVP
Attract higher- quality salespeople	iPod and 1:1 coaching for new hires	• Use of iPod is leading edge and creates a better-selling environment • 1:1 coaching ramps new people faster	• For new salesperson and company, make more sales to make more money (included above) • Less turnover of sales-people provides better customer service and cli-ent retention • Keep one more customer a year = $50,000 • Less turnover costs the company less in recruiting fees and (retrain 3 fewer salespeople a year which saves $100,000)	• Better salespeople create a better image and competi-tive advantage for future products and services
Customer investment	$35,000		$215,000 BENEFIT	

Example of Creating and Defining a Training Solution for a VP of Sales

Another way of figuring out and expressing the benefits of your offering is to brainstorm by putting prospects' priorities and decision criteria in the middle of a page and have them draw spokes out of it as demonstrated in Figure 7.1: R.E.A.L. Brainstorm Your Solution. This is a fun and different way—(If you are really good with PowerPoint you can start with the middle circle and then "build" your benefits click by click. This can also be done very effectively via hand on a piece of paper or whiteboard.)

Figure 7.1
R.E.A.L. Brainstorm Your Solution

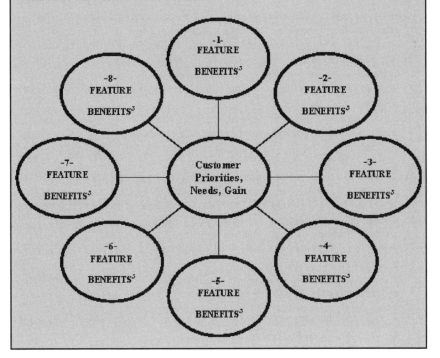

minipresentation and should be related back with benefits to the customers' priorities, needs, and personal gain.

If you are using PowerPoint or Keynote from Apple and are going to hand out copies of your presentation in advance, print your presentation using the "Notes Page" setting so people can take notes which will enhance your presentation. Don't repeat or read what a slide says: interpret its meaning in relation to your audience. If you are concerned they will skip to the end to see the price, don't include it in the handouts. A rule of thumb some people use is ten slides and twenty minutes to present them.

Slide tips: Never have more than five bullets on a slide (and that may be too many). Don't write complete sentences, but rather conceptual "bullets." Use 30-point font for your bullets. If the words don't fit, rework your point!

Some people say only use images that represent or symbolize what you are trying to get across.

Involve the audience: Keep the audience involved by:

- Walking the room. Don't stay in one place.
- Asking their thoughts.
- Having them participate, especially in a demo.
- Giving them exercises to do as part of your presentation.

Enthusiastically (but not fanatically) greet your audience as they trickle in and introduce yourself with your business card in hand. Use appropriate stance, volume, inflection, and gestures. Turn your cell phone off.

Break your presentations into a high-level executive summary and then a more detailed, in-depth presentation, followed by a summary. In other words: Tell 'em what you're gonna tell 'em, tell them, and then tell 'em what you told them!

Always know the roles of the people in the room. Make sure you know what the decision maker cares about and present to that first. When you introduce the people on your team, do so as if they were guest speakers. It builds their credibility.

Keep in mind that stories, anecdotes, and analogies breathe life into a presentation (more later). If you have a "coach" in an account (someone you trust and wants you to win), have that person preview and critique your presentation prior to actually delivering it.

A sense of humor can be a very powerful presentation tool if it isn't used too often and if it doesn't make you sound flippant or not serious. Smile and have fun ... sell them!

Use props or handouts that people can touch and feel while you present. Different people are stimulated in different ways.

Use the acronyms and terms of the prospect's company or industry. It is a huge credibility builder. Provide return on investment (ROI) and references so it is more believable.

Don't forget DiSC when you are presenting. It is crucial. When presenting one to one, be aware of different DiSC styles and adjust accordingly. When presenting to a group, always address the priorities and needs of the decision maker first, and do so in a High Di mode (big picture and results) before going into details and specifics. Less is more. Don't be overdependent on data.

Discuss benefits and make points forcefully: People are motivated to take action if they can see how something will get them what they want (benefits) or avoid what they don't want. With key points, use F.U.D. (fear-uncertainty-doubt). For example you would say, "This is a critical feature and without it you are running a risk of ..." or "Customers have told us that without this ..."

Speak clearly and articulate each word. Know what one message you most want your listeners to remember. Get them to tell you one to three things (your choice) they will walk away with when they leave.

Number your key points, be concise and concrete, and provide a conclusion. Don't be afraid of silence after making an important point.

Present a solution using one of the methods shown in this chapter. Park or place objections on a flip chart as they come up so that they will not take you away from the flow or impact of your presentation. Keep their issues up on the flip chart and cross them off as you address them.

Use the Presentation Planner in the Appendix to help you organize your presentations or demonstrations. And don't forget—there is always a next step after the presentation. Ask the prospect to commit to something.

A Good Proposal Outline

Below is a good outline to use for a written proposal:

- Cover letter
- Table of contents
- Review and confirm understanding of current situation
- Key company attributes and benefits
- Your solution including benefits
- Show your ROI and TTV
- Provide references or case studies
- Define next steps including terms, trial close

R.E.A.L. TIPS AND REMINDERS

☑ Get their attention with a dramatic start.
☑ Introduce your people and their accomplishments. They are buying your company which is people.
☑ Have the prospect introduce his or her people.
☑ Give an overview of the agenda.
☑ Adjust for the environment.
☑ Adjust for the DiSC style.
☑ Brainstorm for solutions. Try to create something unique.
☑ Present your solution.
☑ Check that you are addressing the customer's priorities, needs, and gains.
☑ Practice makes perfect.
☑ Make sure you have next steps mapped out.
☑ Don't line-item the prices of your proposals. Show all the components, but just give a single price for the whole thing. This puts you in a better position when negotiating.
☑ Make sure all proposals have a time that the offer expires. This can push people to make a faster decision, and you can always extend it if you wish.

☑ If your proposal is lengthy, make sure to have a table of contents so people can go where they want and not be intimidated by its size.

☑ Always customize your presentations and proposals to the opportunity.

☑ Always do a spell and grammar check. If it is a big proposal or presentation, have someone double check. I have lost deals because I failed to do this.

☑ If you will be making a PDF out of a document, check page endings. A proposal is a reflection of you and your company. If it looks good, then your services or products look good.

☑ Try to always present proposals versus sending them.

8

Anticipating and Handling Objections

Unfortunately, no matter how good a job you do throughout the sales process, people will have objections. Objections are a natural part of people's buying process. You shouldn't be surprised, upset, or unprepared for them. In fact, it is often a sign of interest, so you should be open to them when they occur. Objections can start to appear at the beginning of the sales process (Stage 2) when you are trying to get an appointment and go all the way through the negotiation and close (Stage 5). Our job as salespeople is to anticipate, soften, and handle objections as best we can throughout the sales cycle so people are ready to buy when we ask them to.

CATEGORIES

To a large measure, based on how well or poorly you use the principles in this book, as well as how good your offering is, people will be in one of three categories when you try to overcome their objections:

Not Interested, No Way

This probably means you shouldn't have been selling to these prospects in the first place but didn't qualify the opportunity early enough using the S.PRI.N.G. Dialogue. Or you might be chasing business that looks big and/or appealing because you don't have enough in your pipeline.

Of course, people can always lie and make you believe they are interested.

I'm Open

This situation occurs often. You want people to be more inclined than less to buy your product or service. This will happen even more often when you follow the steps and use the skills outlined in the book.

I Want You

You probably have done all or most of the right things for this to occur. This will happen more and more often with experience, knowledge, and the application of good selling skills. It will also happen more often if you do many of the things discussed in previous chapters including prospecting to your Sweet Spot, meeting with the right people, building rapport, asking good questions, and making a persuasive presentation.

I learned about these three categories in my first job selling Olivetti typewriters against IBM in 1976. As I mentioned in an earlier chapter, at the time, "Big Blue" had more than 90 percent market share, so there were a lot of people and companies who wouldn't consider my typewriter, even if I showed them it was better and sold it to them for much less money. Two stories stand out vividly. I remember once talking to a Purchasing Manager at a university who had just ordered 120 IBM typewriters to put into storage. I asked him why and he said because you never know when you will be able to get them. The second is when a secretary hugged her typewriter she was so emotionally attached to it. Fortunately, there were plenty of opportunities in the I'm Open and I Want You categories. You need to weed out any and all prospects in the No Way category as early as possible. They are a waste of your time and, unless you have magical powers or can hypnotize people, you will never overcome their objections.

REASONS FOR OBJECTIONS

People have objections for many reasons, many of which we can prevent or soften if we sell properly. These include, but are not limited to:

- They are confused and want to understand something better.
- They don't trust you or like you.
- They prefer another offer.
- You have not done a good job presenting or explaining what they are objecting to.
- They had a bad experience in the past.
- They are using their objection as a smoke screen to what they are really concerned about.
- They want to buy from you, but they are pretending they have objections so they can get a better deal from you.
- They don't want to change or there is a lack of inertia to do so.
- You are talking to the wrong person.
- They legitimately need time to think about it or need to get others involved.
- Your product is too expensive or they don't need everything you are offering.
- They feel safer staying with what they have.
- Changing to what you are selling is too complicated or difficult to do.
- It is somebody else's objection, but they are "toeing" the company line.
- You are competing against a very strong competitor or person (e.g., a board member or relative). This is very difficult to overcome.
- They have other things that are more important.

- You have not shown enough value or difference for them to change or pay what you are asking.
- The competitor is saying things to them and planting their own seeds.

You've probably experienced other objections. Take out a sheet of paper and list them. The following commentary will help you understand how to overcome them in the future.

ANTICIPATING OBJECTIONS

The best way to handle objections is to cut them off at the pass by anticipating them. You can use the form, Table 8.1, to help you prepare.

Some people would say you should let all objections have a voice so you can handle them. I believe the expression "an ounce of prevention is worth a pound of cure" is appropriate here. By getting to the objections before they even break the surface, they won't gain momentum and get any bigger during the sales cycle. The first step in anticipating objections is to delineate what the most common are or might be, and as early as possible in the sales cycle

Table 8.1
R.E.A.L. Objection-Handling Form

STEP IN PROCESS	RESPONSE
Don't Overreact	
Acknowledge with Empathy	
"Piece of Cake" Questions	
Response	
Verify/Trial Close	

(while prospecting or in your first meeting) do or say something to address them. For example, if you know that a common objection is that your product is more expensive than the competition, you might try the following during the sales process:

While prospecting:

- Only prospect to people who can afford a more expensive product or service.
- When someone picks up the phone say, "My name is ... and I am only calling companies that offer premium products themselves."

During the S.PRI.N.G. Dialogue:

- Ask how important price is to them in their decision.
- Ask about their budget to see if they are even in the ballpark of what your offer costs.
- See if they have always bought at the lowest price.
- Ask how they see their own company in terms of the competition—better and worth it or cheaper.
- You might just be very direct and say, "We are usually about x percent more expensive. Will that be a concern or problem?"
- Ask them how much more they would be willing to pay to get exactly what they want.

During the Presentation:

- Discuss and demonstrate the benefits, value, and differences of your product or service prior to presenting your price.
- Offer references of people who had bought despite the price difference.
- Break the price down to its lowest common denominator (more on this later).
- Discuss different financing options if you have them.

As President of IPG, when I am selling to a prospect who is looking at a bigger company, I will ask a certain seed question in the S.PRI.N.G. Dialogue: "Do you prefer a company that is large, but not so large that they cannot customize their program [which bigger companies don't do as well as IPG does]?" Or, I will simply ask what size of a company they have chosen in the past and prefer to work with. Finally, I will ask them where they stand in terms of size versus their competition and why people buy them even though they are smaller. When I present or propose my solution, one of my first slides is all the big companies I have worked with. One of my favorite slides and sayings (which I got from one of my customers years ago) is "Bigger isn't better. Better is better." That lets them know that size has nothing to do with quality. Sometimes I will make an analogy between a big company and a smaller company that provides a much better product or service.

You can see that even if you haven't completely removed the objection, you certainly have softened it in case it comes up again. If it does come up again, it means they are still interested but have a concern. Why else would they keep bringing it up rather than just walking away from you?

FIVE STEPS TO HANDLING OBJECTIONS MORE EFFECTIVELY

1. Don't overreact
2. Acknowledge with empathy
3. Piece of cake questioning
4. Respond
5. Trial close

Don't Overreact

A common mistake that too many salespeople make when they hear an objection is to overreact and start talking, explaining, and defending themselves or their product. They are afraid that the objection is a sign that they will lose the sale (which it may or may not be). This creates defensiveness on the part of the prospect and doesn't allow for an openness or discussion about the objection.

Our job as salespeople is to keep perspective, stay cool, and not let the prospect suck us into their objection. In all cases, your response must be related to what they told you was important from the S.PRI.N.G. Dialogue and/or their DiSC style.

Again, objections can actually be signs of interest, a way for a prospect to ask questions and get clarification on something important to them. If we jump down their throat or say something that doesn't even relate to their objection, we can do some real damage.

Stay calm and try not to talk. Try to listen and understand why this objection is occurring. Is it because of the competition, previous experiences, lack of knowledge or trust, the competition, truly not understanding, etc.? Turn on your empathic listening and listen for words and feelings.

Acknowledge with Empathy

I call this the Bill of Rights of objections. People have the right to object. They should object to make the best decision for themselves, their companies, or their families. You should support their right to have objections by acknowledging that you heard them and their objection. Keep your acknowledgment simple and don't overcomplicate your response.

You might say with sincere empathy and appreciation:

- I appreciate that.
- Thanks for your honesty.
- I appreciate you sharing that with me.

- That is a good question at this point.
- Others have felt similarly before buying our solution.
- Others have felt similarly at this stage of the process.
- Thank you.
- That is an excellent question.

Try NOT to say:

- I agree.
- You are right.
- I feel the same way.
- I understand.

These all agree or imply that you agree with the prospect's objection and make it harder to come back with a legitimate response (especially with a mean High D or Dominant behavior style). The only time you should agree is when a customer or prospect tells you they had a bad experience with your company, product, etc. In this instance you should say, "I am sorry that happened. Please tell me more."

Acknowledging is a powerful tool. A few stories can illustrate it best.

True Story 1

I was going on a research call with one of my customers in Canada who sold audio conferencing (where many people speak to each other over a service or audio bridge). We were visiting one of their best customers (a mining company) that had been using my customer's service for three years to hold their quarterly Investor Relations calls. These are very important and prestigious calls to the investment community where the CEO, CFO, and others discuss their strategies and earnings. They can directly affect the price of their stock and also how easily and affordably they can borrow money.

The salesperson for this account was telling me these calls had been perfect, never a glitch, and we were visiting the CEO's office to meet his new Personal Assistant (PA) and schedule the next call. Needless to say he was very relaxed and confident. The receptionist greeted us and brought us into a conference room that was worth more than the gross national product of some countries. While we waited for the PA we were brought tea and coffee in the finest china. Finally the new PA came and after pleasant introductions said to the salesperson, "I know you have done a good job but I think I am going to look at other providers." I know my jaw dropped so I can only imagine how he felt. Instead of overreacting and getting defensive, which 99.9 percent of the salespeople in the world would have done, he said "I appreciate you letting me know. Thank you." Well if you could see a mood change in the room, you would have. Everything softened when he said that. She was probably nervous telling him and was expecting the usual retort and defensiveness. Her whole demeanor changed and by the end of the meeting, he walked out with the order for the next call.

True Story 2

I had a good relationship with a customer for about six months, and all of a sudden it turned sour. I had no idea why. She wouldn't return my calls or emails, and we had planned to do some business for a President's Club (an incentive trip for her salespeople). This went on for more than three months and I was worried.

Finally I got to her and said, "Janice, I can't help but notice that something has happened to our relationship. May I ask what?" She got very angry, started to berate me personally, and told me I had done something that she didn't approve of. I was rattled but I remembered the process and said, "Janice, I can't tell you I like hearing what you are saying, but I do appreciate you letting me know. Can we discuss this so we can try and get past this?" By not reacting to her anger, she softened a bit and we were able to clear the air a bit. Not totally, but it was a beginning.

"Piece of Cake" Questioning

You'll recall from our previous discussion of this topic, the term *piece of cake* means easy. Also, if you cut a round cake, a piece of it will be broad and then narrow down to a tip. After acknowledging the objection, the first question you should ask is very open ended. Then let the customer speak. After that, ask questions that narrow down what the customer's real concern is on a product, business/financial, and personal level and plant seeds to establish how you will respond. Some questions or probes you could start with (again with empathy and a desire to understand) are:

- May I ask you some questions to understand this better?
- Please, tell me more.
- Why is that a concern?
- What concerns you about this?

Questions that narrow down are:

- Do you like what we have been discussing or showing you? May I ask what in particular? (This is especially effective during a negotiation.)
- Do you have any other concerns besides the one you just mentioned? (This is essential during a negotiation.)
- Can you tell me exactly what your concern is?
- May I ask why this is coming up now?
- Is this your concern or others' as well? Who else shares this concern with you?
- If we were to put your concern aside for one moment, would you go with us? If so, why?

Tip: A good thing to do if the prospect is allowing you to ask several questions is to acknowledge them for doing so. This will allow you to ask even more questions and plant seeds for your response.

Respond

Notice that responding is the fourth step, not the first, which is what most salespeople do. If done properly, you understand the objection and have set up your response via Steps 2 and 3.

There are six primary ways to respond, and multiple combinations of these six you can use depending upon the situation, your relationship, and how emotional the objection is. Note that there are some objections you can't apply all these responses to:

- *Direct:* Best used with High D's or C's, when there is a strong relationship, and there have been very few obstacles. Also good when the objection is less emotional or subjective and more factual.
- *Analogy:* Good for High i's or S's. Excellent way of setting the stage to give them some direct information or bring them to a place where they experience the objection they have in a positive way. Good for emotional objections.
- *Big Picture or Forest for the Trees:* Good for all DiSC styles. This is best used when the objection is real, but you want to put into perspective bigger priorities or issues the prospect or customer has told you. You might ask permission from the Ds and Cs so they don't think you are being evasive or indirect.
- *U-Turn:* Good for i and S DiSC styles. Best used when you need to shock someone into listening to you. This response starts by telling a person that their concern or objection is the reason they should buy from you versus not buy from you. Good when there is a lot of resistance.
- *It Could Be Worse:* Good for all DiSC styles except D. Sometimes referred to as a F.U.D. response (Fear, Uncertainty, and Doubt), you respond by telling people things could be worse if they don't go with you or things could be worse than the objection they have. Good for emotional objections.
- *The Politician's Response:* I include this because it seems to work in some cases. In this instance, you basically don't respond to their objection and bring them to the point you want to make, just like politicians.

These responses can also be types of questions during Stage 3 of this process. For example, you might ask customers what they have done in the past when they had to address the same concern they have now. This is an Analogy question. Or you could ask prospects what would be the worst scenario they can imagine if they don't have what you are selling. This is an It Could Be Worse question as well as a F.U.D. seed. Asking customers if the priorities and needs they had told you about earlier are still relevant is an example of a Big Picture question.

Trial Close

After you respond, you need to see if the customer is OK or if you need to go back to Step 3. If it is late enough in the sales cycle, you can also trial close. Some examples are:

- Are we OK?
- Do you feel better?
- Do you agree?
- If I have addressed your concern, can we place your order?
- Have I answered your question?

We'll cover more trial closes in Chapter 9.

SAMPLE SCENARIOS

Price Objections

First, of course, acknowledge: "Thank you for being so honest with me. I appreciate it."

Questions

Piece of Cake:

- May we discuss this?
- Are there any other concerns?
- Please tell me more.

Narrowing:

- Is it the overall price or the initial fee?
- How much more expensive?
- Is this in comparison to something else?
- Is it in comparison to your budget?
- Are you not sure what you are getting or that you need what we have proposed?
- What have you done in the past when you wanted something, but it was more expensive?
- Is there anything you would want us to take out?
- If we could make you feel more comfortable with the price, would you be able to place an order?
- If we could spread the payments out, would that help?
- I am curious, are you least expensive in your industry? Why do people pay more for you?
- How does this relate to your priorities? Have they changed?

Analogy Response

"Mr./Ms. Prospect, just like you, we are not the least expensive, but we offer a quality product and service that more than justifies the price and will help you address the priorities and needs we have discussed.''

Other analogies you can use are:

- Home or car insurance
- Healthcare insurance
- Buying a car
- Deciding on a school for your kids
- Picking a vacation or airline
- Others?

Big Picture or Forest for the Trees Response

''Mr./Ms. Prospect, money is a very emotional subject. It is for me as well when I make important business decisions. If you know the expression 'the forest for the trees,' we are standing right in front of the money tree, and we can't see the forest of things you wanted and benefits we bring. If we can take a step back and remind ourselves of all your priorities, the things you wanted and reasons you wanted to change, we might have a better perspective.''

The opposite of the Big Picture is to break the price difference into its smallest component. Here is an example:

You: ''How much more expensive are we?''
Prospect: ''20 percent''
You: ''What does 20 percent mean in dollars?''
Prospect: ''$400''
You: ''How long do you expect to use our product?''
Prospect: ''One year.''
You: ''So if we are to break that down by day that is $1.09 a day ($400 divided by 365 days), which is less than you probably spend on a cup of coffee. Let me remind you what you get for that $1.09....''

If you are selling a product or service that helps somebody save or make money, you can go even further and break it down by hour:

You: ''If we were to break that difference down by an eight-hour working day, that is twenty-six cents an hour.''

If it is a deductible business expense:

You: ''If you are in a 30 percent tax bracket, you can take another 7.8 cents off (30 percent of twenty-six cents) so the total difference for everything we are offering is eighteen cents an hour.''

U-Turn Response

"Mr./Ms. Prospect, this might sound a bit odd, but your concern is actually the reason most of our customers buy from us because it gives them the assurance they are getting exactly what they want which in your case would be...."

"Mr./Ms. Prospect, I hope you don't take this the wrong way, but your concern is actually the reason you should buy from us because it means you are getting everything you want. The easiest thing is to reduce price but we don't think that will help you."

"Mr./Ms. Prospect, I hope you take this the right way, but because you are asking me why we are so expensive would you please ask the competition why they are less expensive?"

"Mr./Ms. Prospect, one of two things is happening. We are either taking advantage of you or something is missing from the competitor's offers. And we know that our offer is worth it. More important, we know it will help you...."

It Could Be Worse

"Based on what you have told me, the only situation that I can think of that would be worse then spending $400 more dollars is if the less-expensive product doesn't address your priorities and needs. That will cost you a lot more than $400."

"It is possible that the price is going to go up because of demand, production costs, etc. so it is possible that it could be even more expensive if you don't buy now."

The Politician's Response

"I know we are $400 more expensive but let's get back to the main point, which is your priorities and...."

Verify/Trial Close (for any type of response):

- Does that answer your question?
- Do you feel more comfortable now?
- Can we place your order?
- If you don't have any other questions, can we start the paperwork?

If they don't agree at this point, acknowledge their no and ask if you can discuss it further. Try to avoid getting more adamant and emotional.

Resistance to Change or Happy with Current Status Objections

Questions

Piece of cake:

- May we discuss this? Are there any other concerns? Please tell me more.

Narrowing:

- When we spoke you told me you had these concerns about your current situation. Have those changed?
- What has happened since we last spoke that you are so concerned?
- Is your concern more about what is needed to change, not knowing how we would do it, or if it is just worth it?
- Please tell me how you have changed in the past that was a positive and easy experience (an analogy question).
- Is there any aspect of changing in particular you are concerned with?
- Give me your worst scenario so we can see if we can address it (it could be worst question).
- If I may ask, is there anybody else who shares this concern?
- Do you still see the benefits of our offer but the change is concerning you? (Forest from Trees question)

Analogy Responses

"Change is something that happens all the time. If we could replicate a change you have had in the past that was positive, would we be able to move forward?"

"I had a customer in the same situation. He had exactly the same concern and here is how we handled it...."

"Change is not easy. It is natural to be resistant to change. At the same time, change is when things get better on a personal and business level. I remember [and then tell them a story when you were scared to change but happier that you did]."

"We had almost the exact situation with Company XYZ and what we did there was...."

"Mr./Ms. it has been our experience that the greater the change, the more important it is to do so. Little problems are easy to change and don't matter as much if you do or don't. An analogy would be if you have bad plumbing. You could do nothing and get by, or, you could address the problem, so it doesn't get any bigger."

Big Picture or Forest for the Trees Response

"Change is always scary and it can cloud our thinking and prevent us from doing what is needed. Let's go back to the things you said you wanted to achieve and if we can break down how we would do it in easy, safe steps, maybe that will make it less overwhelming."

"The most important thing is to keep focused on what you wanted to do and make sure the changes you are concerned with are addressed."

U-Turn

"Mr./Ms. it has been our experience that the greater the change, the more important it is to do so. Little problems are easy to change and don't matter as much if you do or don't. But when you have to make substantial changes, like those we have discussed, it usually means there is a big problem which is exactly why you should move ahead."

It Could Be Worse

"Mr./Ms., the only situation that we can imagine would be worse is if you don't address it now, just imagine how much bigger and worse it is going to be later down the road. Let's find a way to transition you now so that doesn't happen."

Politician's Response

"The bigger issue is that you have to change or you will never be able to do it later. We must do it now."

Verify/Trial Close (for any type of response):

- Does that answer your question?
- Do you feel more comfortable now?
- Can we place your order?
- If you don't have any other questions, can we start the paperwork?

R.E.A.L. TIPS AND REMINDERS

☑ Start in your "Sweet Spot" and you will have fewer objections.
☑ Don't lose sight of all the things you were told and have done prior to the objection. Salespeople get nervous and forget to put the person's objection into the larger context of their priorities, goals, etc.
☑ Don't forget people can be objecting for many reasons, including that they are interested and want to know more.
☑ Avoid just answering when you hear an objection and ask some questions to truly understand their concern.
☑ Use questions and seeds to set up your response.
☑ Never forget DiSC or S.PRI.N.G. when asking questions and responding.
☑ If you know you are going into a stage of the sales cycle where you will get objections (presenting, negotiating, closing), take time to analyze what they might be and how you will handle them.
☑ The customer has the right to make objections. Don't try to persuade or bully them into thinking they don't.
☑ Being empathetic to their concerns and putting yourself in their shoes will raise the level of your questions and responses. The prospect will react in kind.
☑ If a customer allows you to ask several questions, you should thank her for doing so since she didn't need to. This will usually allow you to ask more questions.

9

Closing the Sale

If there were a Hall of Fame for salespeople, and you closed 30 percent of your deals, you would be a candidate. A 40 percent close rate is a sure first ballot entry, and at 50 percent, they would dedicate a wing to you.

MAKE CLOSING EASY

Some of the biggest deals I have ever closed happened when I was away on vacation. Why? Because I did all the right things during the sales cycle so the close happened very easily and naturally. (Perhaps you and I should always go on vacation when working big deals!) This includes all the things we have already discussed in the previous chapters, including:

- Selling into your "Sweet Spot" as much as possible.
- Doing a S.PRI.N.G. Dialogue with the people involved in the decision, especially executives or people in positions of authority.
- Building rapport and developing trust during the sales cycle.
- Presenting your offer in a compelling way that shows your differences and the benefits of your offer.
- Handling objections throughout the sales cycle.
- Being responsive to the prospect throughout all stages.

Even then, you won't close everything. Conversely, no matter how good a "closer" you are, if the right things are not done throughout the sales cycle, you can still close deals, but you will close fewer.

Making a sale—it can't be stressed enough—is a process, not an event. Too many salespeople think of closing as only asking for the deal at the end, which is of course nonetheless essential. This is scary for many salespeople: I know I was afraid to ask for the close as a young salesperson. That aside, it is just as important for salespeople to be closing throughout the sales process, to keep a sale moving forward from one stage to another, and to keep people focused on your product or service, versus another's. An important psychological rule of getting people to say "yes" when you do ask for the order is to have had the prospect take action and invest themselves as much as possible during the sales cycle. The more they are invested, the more difficult it is to back away or to say "no."

So let's define *closing* as the act of asking someone to do something. It could be little, like responding to an e-mail or question. Or it could be big, like asking to visit the prospect in his office or home (if you are selling that type of product), meet your family members (if you are selling something that a family can use), have a meal with you, or introduce you to his boss in a professional setting. Closing is done all the time, regardless of the communications medium (in person, over the phone, e-mail, etc.).

When is the first time you close? At the very beginning when you ask for an appointment. And the last? When you ask for the deal or negotiate the final item!

This chapter discusses:

- Keeping people focused on your offering through a series of actions and commitments called T.E.E.M.™ (time, energy, emotion, money).
- Understanding the power of trial closing.
- Identifying and responding to buying signals, warning signals, and hidden objections.
- Knowing different types of closing techniques, when to use them, and which techniques work best with different DiSC styles.

After this section, you will feel more comfortable with and better able to close more business.

KEEPING PEOPLE FOCUSED ON YOUR OFFERING THROUGH T.E.E.M.

People have a difficult time walking away from things they have invested in. I use the term *T.E.E.M.* which means:

- Time
- Energy
- Emotion
- Money

I use the two following scenarios with my students to demonstrate the point:

Scenario 1: Imagine you are not married (if you really aren't then you don't have to imagine this) and last night you and your loved one decided to get married. Congratulations! You set a date nine months away (let's say April 28). You choose to follow a more traditional course of events, including:

- Calling your parents.
- Telling all your friends.
- Choosing the place you would have the ceremony and the party.

- Picking the food, decorations, music, flowers, etc.
- Picking the best man and maid of honor.
- Introducing families to each other.
- Having a rehearsal dinner.
- Spending a lot of money on an engagement ring.

Scenario 2: Now let's imagine the same event but you decided to keep it quiet. You still set the date of April 28 but no calls to family or friends, no formal plans—just a simple ceremony at City Hall. So—in either scenario—the big day comes and you are naturally excited and nervous. This is a big decision you are making. You love the person, but do you really want to be with this person, and only this person, for the rest of your life? Are you making a mistake? You start to get cold feet. In which scenario do you think it would be easier to back out or delay the decision: the first or second?

The answer is Scenario 2, of course, because you didn't take as many actions to commit yourself to the event. It is easier to walk away or delay because you didn't do very much anyway. (I like to think they still get married in the second scenario, but it's when they have time on their busy schedules.) Can you think of a time you were involved in a situation where it was hard to back out of because of the commitments you had made, or easy because you hadn't? If you can, then you will understand the power of this concept.

In the world of sales, we need to create reasons or situations for people to invest their T.E.E.M. The way we do this is by getting prospects to commit to a series of events, some easy to invest in and commit to, others more difficult. The most difficult is the final "yes," where they sign a purchase agreement and give you their money. If you can get prospects to commit to you while you are selling to them you are increasing the probability of winning more sales. The first step is by defining the actions or T.E.E.M. a person would take at each stage of the sales process.

Below is an example of a sales process, where I have defined the T.E.E.M./actions the prospect will take (they are in italics) during a sales cycle (and mixed in with their own approach) to increase my chances of making a sale:

1. Identify and gain access to the decision maker.
2. Do a S.PRI.N.G. Dialogue.
3. *Allow me to interview other people in the company to get their input using the S.PRI.N.G. Dialogue.*
4. *Have the prospects send me some information about their products, competition, current sales figures, and more.*
5. *Agree to read or have me present a draft proposal—in person or via Web.*
6. *Agree to review my contract.*
7. *Have client visit or call references.*
8. *Agree to read or hear my final proposal—in person or over Web.*
9. Close, or negotiate and close.

I try to get commitment to all steps, but I win most often when people will commit to Steps 3–7 because these show a commitment of time, energy, and emotion on the prospect's part. If I can do any of these steps in my office or a place they have to travel to (visit references), then I get them to commit money as well. I have to close people to do these steps. If they do, I win more business.

A great way to do this with the customers is to ask them what their buying process is and then overlay your steps to see if you can get them to commit. Think of it as a selling time line that you and the customer agree to. Figure 9.1 is a selling Time Line. The items below the line represent the customer's buying process. The items above the line represent the steps I want them to take to get more T.E.E.M. from them.

Figure 9.1
Selling Time Line

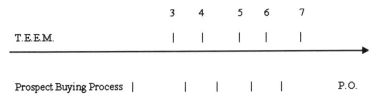

Do you know your ideal method to get T.E.E.M.? If not, take some time to define it and how you will get people to commit.

OTHER WAYS TO GET T.E.E.M.

There are many ways to get T.E.E.M. from your prospects and customers.

- Send them articles to read.
- Ask them for information to send to you.
- Take them out to a meal.
- Socialize.
- Ask them to introduce you to other people.
- Introduce them to other people who can help them reach goals.
- Send a draft proposal.
- Do a demonstration.
- Have them come to your office for any of the above business items.
- Have them talk to your references.
- Send them something that they like on a personal level.
- Ask them for technical information you need to put your proposal or presentation together.
- Have them show you their offices or facilities.
- If you have executives, have them invite the prospects' executives out to dinner or for an appointment.

THE POWER OF TRIAL CLOSING

Trial closing (getting a read on how a situation is going, something you said, or even asking for the order) is a critical skill when selling and should be used for many reasons throughout the sales process. One is to test the waters to see how you are doing at any stage and whether people are agreeing with you. This is especially important if you are presenting over the phone or via web conferencing and you have no visual input telling you if they like what you are doing.

Another is to see if prospects will do something you want them to do to move the sale forward. For example, you might want to trial close:

- To flush out objections.
- To have them talk to you.
- When you hear a buying signal.
- At the appropriate time, to ask for the sale.

Some examples of trial closes are:

- Do you agree?
- What are your thoughts?
- How would you like to proceed?
- So ....?
- Can you see how this will work for you?

Some examples of how you would trial close on some of the items we mentioned in T.E.E.M. are shown in Table 9.1.

Finally, use a trial close to see if the prospect is ready to say "yes" and buy from you. "Can I write up the order now?"

Trial Closes at the End of the Sales Process

Example A:

Prospect: "You have put together a very attractive proposal."
Salesperson: "Thank you very much. Unless you have any other questions, I was hoping we could get the contract signed and deliver this to you." (Trial close)

Example B:

Prospect: "How much is this going to save me?" (Buying signal)
Salesperson: "Well based on our conversation, it will be around $250/month. Do you want to get going?" (Trial close)

Look for Buying Signals

A buying signal is a sign of interest and comes in many forms, including verbal, physical, and emotional. When you identify a buying signal, you should finish what you are doing and trial close, not just provide information. For example, if a prospect says, "That sounds interesting," you would

Table 9.1
Trial Closes to Generate T.E.E.M.

Idea	Trial Close
Send them articles to read.	Would you be willing to read some articles written about this?
Ask them for information to send to you.	Can you send me the information so we can put a proposal together for you?
Take them out to a meal.	What is the best time for us to meet?
Ask them to introduce you to other people.	It would be great to meet others involved. What is the best way to do this?
You introduce them to other people.	We would love for you to meet some of the key people in our organization. Can we have you come by our offices to do that? What would be the best day?
Send a draft proposal.	I think it best to send a draft and have us both go over it before we send a final. How does that sound to you?
Do a demonstration.	A demonstration would really answer a lot of your questions. When can we set it up?
Have them come to your office for any of the above business items.	The best place to do this is at our facilities. Can we have you and the others involved come visit us?
Talk to references.	We have several clients that were in a similar position to yours. Would you like to speak with them?
Send them something that they like on a personal level.	Would it be OK if I sent you something? Where should I send it to?
Ask them for technical information you need to put your proposal or presentation together.	We need your current configurations to do a proposal. Who is the best person to speak with and get that from? Is it possible for you to set that up?
Having them show you their offices or facilities.	Can you show us your facilities?
If you have executives, have them invite the prospects out to dinner or a social event.	My VP would like to invite you and your boss to a social event we sponsor. Are you open to that?

say, "Great, I am glad you can see how valuable this would be for you. Can we get going?" This way you get the prospect to say "yes," or reveal what else they need to know/hear to say "yes."

Additional buying signals and trial closes are outlined in Table 9.2.
Additional buying signals include:

- If you are selling to more than one person, they start talking about how they can use your product.
- They call you about something or call often.
- They run out of questions to ask.
- Their demeanor changes from very intense to very relaxed.
- They start nodding and agreeing with what you are saying.
- They want to introduce you to others involved in the buying process.
- They return your e-mails and phone mails sooner than they had been.

Remember this rule: If you hear a buying signal, finish what you are saying or doing, answer their question, and trial close. Don't just answer the

Table 9.2
How to Handle Buying Signals

Buying Signal	Trial Close
• How long will it take us to actually get this installed or deliver it?	• Usually about 3–4 weeks (answer). If that works for you can we place your order (trial close).
• Thank goodness you mentioned this to us. We have been looking for something like this a long time.	• I am glad you are so excited (answer/respond). Let's get going then (trial close).
• You've done a great job.	• Thank you. I appreciate it. Unless you have other questions, can we start the paperwork?
• Tell me more about this capability.	• Sure, it does X, Y, and Z. If that answers your question, maybe we can get going.
• What colors does it come in?	• 23 different colors. If we have the color you want, would you be ready to place an order?
• How much is it?	• It is $400. Would you like to order one?
• Can I see your contract?	• Of course. Are there any particular areas you want to cover before we sign?
• Can you do better on the pricing?	• Probably not, but I might be able to add some extras. Would that get us over the hurdle so you can sign?

question. That is a common mistake that many salespeople make. For example:

Prospect: "Have you sold this to anyone else in my industry?"
Salesperson: "Yes, I have to Company A, B, and C."

Better:

Prospect: "Have you sold this to anyone else in my industry?"
Salesperson: "Yes, I have sold to Company A, B, and C and they are all very happy. I would love to add you to that list. Can I send you our contract?"

Identify and Respond to Warning Signals

If a buying signal is a sign of interest, then a warning signal is a sign of concern on the prospect's part, and that means you need to be concerned as well. Warning signals are not as obvious or overt as an objection, but if you hear or observe a warning signal, finish what you are doing and handle it as if it were an objection. For example, a prospect says:

Prospect: "This seems a bit of overkill" (If stated as an objection it would be more obvious, like "I don't need all this.")
Salesperson: "I appreciate your honesty. Can you tell me a bit more? Is it the whole proposal or just certain parts?"

Here is a list of possible warning signals:

- I am not sure.
- This seems a bit of overkill.
- We have to think about it.
- You hear the prospect answering e-mails or shuffling papers while you are talking on the phone.
- The prospect takes a call from someone else while you are talking to her.
- The prospect has lots of stuff from your competitor in her office.
- The prospect uses the language and acronyms of the competition.
- The prospect says, "I have to talk to others and see how they feel."
- The prospect says, "You all seem pretty much the same."
- The prospect doesn't respond to your questions, e-mails, or voicemails.
- The prospect cancels appointments.

Again, work to find out what the issue is, then address it.

Identify and Respond to Hidden Objections

Hidden objections are concerns people have but disguise them as well-intended or simple questions. They do this for many reasons including:

- They don't want to show their cards by stating their concern as clearly as an objection.

- They are testing your integrity and honesty against something they already know.
- They favor the competition and are setting you up to look bad.

Be on the lookout for hidden objections toward the end of the sale or when new people are introduced and don't want to show their cards. You might also see these from people you know favor your competition.

You handle hidden objections by giving a bit of information and then asking a question.

True Story

I was presenting to a group of six vice presidents of a company who sold three different pieces of equipment. Coincidentally, I was presenting three of my training programs: sales, customer service, and management. The presentation was going extremely well. So well in fact that the senior vice president (SVP) got suspicious and the following conversation ensued:

SVP: "Jon, of the three things you are presenting and want us to buy, which one are you best at?" [His real concern or objection was "I don't believe you can do all of these things as well as you say."]

Me: "Jay, that is an interesting question. Why do you ask?" [Acknowledge and ask a question.]

SVP: "Jon, everyone is coming in and pitching us for all of our business, but I don't believe anyone can do everything as well as they say." [He reveals his real concern.]

Me: "Is that all? Do you have any other questions?"

SVP: "No."

Me: "Jay, I am not sure how to answer that except by answering you with a question. When are your customers better off? When they buy one of your products or when they buy all three that work together in unison?" [This is an example of the Analogy response.]

SVP: "When they buy all three."

Me: "Jay, I am the same as you. All of my programs are very good, but they are even better when they work together."

He had no other concerns, and I won the business.

DIFFERENT CLOSING TECHNIQUES

There are many closing techniques you can use. As I mentioned in the second paragraph of this chapter, if you haven't done all the right things properly, you won't close as much business no matter how well you deploy some of these techniques. The different types of closings—when they are best used—and with the different personality types—are described in Table 9.3.

Table 9.3
Types of Trial Closings

CLOSE	BEST USED	DiSC® STYLE
President's Club	Best used when you have a good relationship with someone and you tell him you need the deal to win an award or a trip from the company. Example: "Since it appears we will be doing business with each other, would it be OK for you to place your order now so I can make our special President's Club incentive?	All
Limited Supply	When you have limited supply of a hot product, an older product that is going out of production, or a product where production is being slowed down. Document what you are saying. Example: "I don't want to put undue pressure, but we are running low on availability and unless we place your order now, we might run out completely. Can we do that?"	All
Blank or Get off the Pot	When you have a time limit on your offer, person needs a push, or they have been taking forever to make a decision. Example: "Mr. Jones, unless we do something in the next 48 hours, I will assume you are no longer interested."	i, S, C
Promotional Pricing	When available. Example: "Ms. Jones, unless we do something in the next 48 hours, you will lose the special offer and miss your deadline. Can we place your order now?"	All
End of Quarter or Year Close	At end of quarter or year when you can offer special incentives that will go away. Document it for credibility.	All
The Option Close	Offer two equally appealing options; you make a sale in either case. Example: "Ms. Black, you can choose the 1st option which has everything you need now and in the future or the 2nd option which allows you to address your current needs and add on later, at a little bit higher expense. Which do you prefer?"	D, i

(Continued)

Table 9.3
Types of Trial Closings (*Continued*)

CLOSE	BEST USED	DiSC® STYLE
The U-Turn Close	When someone has a strong concern about something. You show them how the thing they are concerned with is actually an advantage. Example: "Being that we are a smaller company means we will give you more attention because of your importance to us. I hope we can begin demonstrating that by signing the agreement. May we?"	i, S
The Comfort Close	Making them as comfortable as possible by reiterating all the great things that will happen in the future once everything is in and working. Example: "So, Jonathan, once we get going you will be able to realize all the things you have told me were important to you—more money, a better house and ability to take care of your family. Can we get started?"	S
The John Lennon Close (Imagine …)	Similar to the Comfort Close except there is less detail and more focus on the imagery of the future. Must be very upbeat and optimistic. Example: "It is exciting to imagine, Jonathan, that you will attain everything you want and more because you are taking the bold step and action of doing something and taking control of your destiny. That is what is possible and we can help you with once you get going. When can we get started?"	S, i
The Direct Close	When you have a good relationship with or things are going extremely well. (But not too direct with a D.) Example: "Susan, can you sign the agreement now so I can schedule this?"	All
Pending Event Close	When the prospect has a pending event and time frame that has to be met. Example "Lucy, I don't want to miss the deadline you told me was so critical to your project. If we don't have the order in by tomorrow, that could happen. Can you sign the contract and get it over to us by then?"	All

Personal Win Close	When it helps them get what they want on a personal gain level.	D, i
	Example: "Sam, you were nice enough to tell me that if this project was successful that you and your people would get the recognition you have been coveting for a long time. Let's not miss that. Can you send the contract over today?"	
The Pros and Cons Close	Use with a logical and methodical thinker, and also someone who is tentative and needs some guidance. This close delineates both the pros and cons of going with your offering. Of course, there should always be more pros than cons, or don't use this close.	S, C
	Example: "Pam, there are pros and cons to any decision. The cons to this are ….. The pros are ….. and I think they far outweigh the cons. I hope you agree and if you do, can we get your P.O. by the end of the day?"	
Silent Close	Very assumptive. Use when you make a strong point or use after trial close. Can also use when things are going well.	All
	Example: "This is the only solution to your problem. I hope you agree."	
Management Close	Bring management in to a meeting to close.	All
	Example: "Jonathan has asked me to see if you have any questions or concerns about us moving forward that I might answer."	
What Do We Have To Do To Get This Thing Closed?	Asking for advice from someone you have worked a long time with or have a good relationship—a very soft close.	i, S
	Example: "Chris, we have done a tremendous amount with each other. What do we need to do to consummate the deal?"	
Instructional Close	"Give us the order and we can proceed"—giving direction to someone who seems confused/hesitant about how to move forward.	S, C

(Continued)

Table 9.3
Types of Trial Closings (*Continued*)

CLOSE	BEST USED	DiSC® STYLE
	Example: "Joe, the way it would work from here is once we get your order, it goes into our manufacturing area and we start to assemble it. About a week later they inform us when it will be ready so we can schedule training. Would you like to set things up by placing your order?"	
Conditional or Buy and Try Close	This is a fantastic way to see if people are really interested and to get a real commitment. Have them sign a "Letter of Intent" or Conditional P.O. that says they can try your product or service for a certain amount of time, after which they buy it, or return it with no, or very little money lost.	All
	Example: "Jeff, by signing this letter of intent, we can put everything in motion that we have agreed to instead of waiting for you to get us a purchase order. Once we do get it, which has to be within two weeks, we will be that much further ahead in the process. Do you want to review and sign this letter?"	
The Puppy Dog Close	This is a sales technique that is based on a method to sell puppies. The idea is to break down the sale into a smaller component with a no-risk offer so the customer will be willing to make an initial commitment.	i, S
	Example: "Sandy, why don't you take the puppy home with you and if you don't like it, just bring it back?" (Knowing they will fall in love with the puppy.)	

R.E.A.L. TIPS AND REMINDERS

☑ The more prepared you are, the better able you will be to detect buying, warning, and hidden signals.

☑ Close for commitment and next steps early in the sale. Get them to give you T.E.E.M.

☑ Don't trial close too early for the deal—you will lose all credibility. However, you should trial close to make sure they are happy with what you are doing and saying early on.

☑ Don't be afraid to close—people know you are there to sell them something, so ask for the order.

☑ Don't be afraid to be quiet after you ask for the close—especially with High S and High C prospects.

☑ You will not close deals where you don't ask for the order.

☑ If you hear silence, it means they are not interested, thinking, or don't need to hear anything else. Trial close to see which it is.

☑ Trial closes will reveal concerns that you should handle as objections. This can accelerate the sales cycle for a faster close.

☑ If you know you are going into a situation to close a deal, decide which closing technique will be best. You should also anticipate objections and prepare for those as well.

10

Negotiating the Deal

Congratulations—almost. You have done everything you should to get to the last and final stage of negotiating and closing the deal. However, it may not go as easily as you hope.

GETTING NERVOUS AND PROTECTIVE

People tend to get nervous and protective during a negotiation and forget everything but what they want. Greed and self-interest set in. They see this stage as the point of "no return" and want to make sure they get everything. This is a very emotional time (for both sides), and it can make people short sighted and prevent them from seeing things objectively.

Our job as salespeople is to prevent this from happening as much as possible by not being "drawn in" to their emotions and tactics. We also want to remember the value of our offer and why we are negotiating in the first place: they want what we are selling or they wouldn't be negotiating with us!

At this point, both parties have more rather than less in common (see Table 10.1) when they are sitting across or around the negotiation table, but they sometimes lose sight of these because of the emotions involved (those in bold being especially emotional).

COMMONALITY

Why do we not see what we have in common? We have not done a good job with the elements listed in Table 10.1. Some of the issues are more emotional than others or have greater repercussions.

Another reason might be that we are negotiating with someone whose job is to work us over in negotiation and get everything possible. This happens a lot with very big companies whose purchasing people are trained to do this. Also, we might let our emotions or DiSC style get in the way. We begin to negotiate too early and the prospect really doesn't

Table 10.1
What Salespeople and Prospects Want, and What They Have in Common

Salesperson/Company	Prospect
A happy customer	A good purchase
A referenceable customer	Good service and support
Growth	Growth
Lack of problems	Lack of problems
Good relations	Good relations
Terms and conditions that protect your company	**Terms and conditions that protect their company**
Volume	Discounts for volume business
A reliable customer	A reliable vendor
A fair and profitable price	**A fair and competitive price**
Protection from litigation	**Protection from misrepresentation**
An easy customer	Worry-free use of the product or service
What others do you experience?	

see the value of our offer. The conditions needed for the sale are not really there. For the sake of discussion, we will use Dictionary.com's definition of the word *negotiate*: ''to deal or bargain with another or others, as in the preparation of a treaty or contract or in preliminaries to a business deal.''

This chapter focuses on how to have negotiations that end up with you and the prospect (soon to be customer) feeling satisfied and maintaining as profitable a business as possible.

FOUR NEGOTIATION STRATEGIES

There are four primary negotiation styles or strategies you (or the customer) can use, depending upon what you are selling and the circumstance or situation you are in:

1. Firm, or Take It or Leave It
2. Too Soft
3. Give/Get (the most common)
4. Bigger Picture

What has occurred in the four prior sales stages has a great affect on what strategy you or the prospect might use, including:

- The level of trust between the negotiating parties (DiSC, commonality, time spent, etc.).
- How well you have planted seeds along the way to anticipate or soften issues so the prospect knows what is or isn't negotiable.
- Not being commoditized and establishing the unique value of your solution.
- Negotiating with the right person or representative of that person who has a real interest (qualified during S.PRI.N.G. Dialogue), and who has confirmed that a real requirement (an impending or compelling event) is driving the sale.
- Whether this is a one-time sale, one that occurs every few years (like buying a car), or the beginning of a longer relationship.
- The size of the deal or follow-up potential.
- The responsibility of the person you are negotiating with.
- If they are an existing customer.
- How strategic they are to you.

Let's now look at each strategy in depth.

Firm, or Take It or Leave It

A "Firm" negotiation strategy is generally used when:

- You are selling a product that has very low margin and/or will occur very infrequently over a long time period.
- You are the only game in town.
- You are selling a product or service with high image or high demand and don't want either of those to diminish either.
- You don't want to set a precedent with a customer by giving her a better price than you have previously.
- The prospect or customer plays it this way.
- You have a lot in the funnel and you would like, but don't need, their business.

Firm Story 1

I had sold my training services to a very hot prospect, and they were satisfied with the program and my pricing. However, I had made a mistake. I did not know that the businessperson I was dealing with would then hand it off to the Purchasing Department, whose mission was to get a better deal. I met with the woman who was responsible for negotiating deals for the business and she started by saying, "I want 25 percent off." I asked her why and she said "Because." I was dumbfounded. I expected a Firm style but not a belligerent style. Being a very High D, I was ready to say "Get lost. No way. You are kidding me" (or something less polite), but I kept my cool and told her she had to give me a better reason than that. She told me that her primary responsibility was to get a better price or she wasn't doing her job. I asked her some questions and decided I would discount the deal further (about 14 percent) because I wanted to get the account. In retrospect, it was a mistake because no matter how good my program was, they always wanted more.

Firm Story 2

This story happened when I was selling Olivetti typewriters against IBM. If you remember from Chapter 4, I had to find industries or applications where I had an advantage over IBM. In this case, I was selling nineteen typewriters to an engineering firm. They asked me for a discount, and I was considering giving it to them, and then I realized they had to have my typewriter. I didn't need to discount, so I said "no" in a very polite and professional way. They bought my nineteen typewriters, were very happy customers, and I was a very happy salesperson.

Too Soft

A "Too Soft" strategy can be used when you want to get an account, or you want to create a beachhead for your company in an industry. You can also use it during tough economic times, or when you provided poor service to a customer and want to make amends. You might also use it when you want to get a large account where there is a lot more opportunity, or when lower margins are made up by higher volumes. Another case where a Too Soft strategy can be used is when you are at the end of your month, quarter, or year and need to bring in revenue.

A Too Soft Story

I wanted to get into a very large company and had been chosen, but I had made a mistake of not knowing the last step in the sales process. I had pretty much been soft throughout the sales process to win the deal. They were merciless in their negotiations. They realized they had me over a barrel so no matter how much I tried, they stuck to their demands and wouldn't give in. I ended up giving in to their price in the hopes I would get more business by proving how great my services were. I got some additional business but never what I had hoped for. Their style of negotiating was an indication they would never be any different and would always shop around. I learned a good lesson and now try to get guarantees on a certain volume to make up for lower prices. Moral of the story: Too soft almost always favors the buyer.

Give/Get

A "Give/Get" strategy is the one most commonly used. You and the prospect give something to get something. For example, you might give a better price if you get a greater volume, or you might give them a quicker delivery if you get the order sooner. One of the most important parts of this strategy is, prior to giving them what they want, to try and come up with an alternative offer to their request that has high value for them and a low cost for you. For example, if you are selling a product and prospects want you to give them a better price, you might offer them more training (which doesn't cost you much) and will allow them to use the product faster and make more money from it.

You should know what alternative offers you might make in preparing for your negotiation and in anticipation of the issues a prospect might have or tactics they might use. Table 10.2 provides some examples.

Bigger Picture

A "Bigger Picture" strategy is used when you and the prospect have truly worked with each other as peers and there is an opportunity to negotiate something bigger than just a buy/sell arrangement. For example, if you are selling a technology to a bank, you could negotiate that you will do all your banking with them. I often suggest to people to think about using this strategy when there are very few obstacles and you and the prospect have been working extremely well with each other.

Bigger Picture Story 1

I recently negotiated a deal with a customer where we shared in the success or failure of the project. We had built enough respect for each other

Table 10.2
Examples of a Give/Get Strategy

Issue	Alternative Offer	Get from Prospect
Better price or % discount	Add more capability or service	The order sooner or a bigger deal
	A smaller order at the same discount %	Get a commitment for the next order

and the value of our respective offerings that we decided to go beyond just a Give/Get. The end result is that they stand to make millions more dollars and I stand to make significantly more than my standard fees.

Bigger Picture Story 2

The second story started at Firm (on the customer's part) and ended in Bigger Picture. When I was with a leading provider of video conferencing, we had been trying to close a very big deal with a retailer who was head-quartered in New York and had thirteen stores in which they wanted to put video. The CIO (Chief Information Officer) had been our main contact, supporter, and saw the value the technology could bring to his company. Unfortunately, he didn't have the budget and couldn't find anyone to spend their own budget. About a year into working with him, we finally thought we had an opportunity so we sent our four-page contract to Purchasing with pricing for this size of a deal, which represented about a 15 percent discount.

A week later I was sitting in front of the Head of Purchasing with a forty-page document that included very harsh terms protecting them and leaving us totally exposed. Page one started out with a request for a minimum of 45 percent discount. I asked the gentleman in front of me whether we could discuss the terms first (hoping we could work our way back to a much lower discount) and he told me that without agreeing on the pricing, we couldn't do business. I stood up, shook his hand, thanked him, and left. This happened for many reasons, including his role, his lack of interest, his not understanding the value of our solution (plus the fact that he was a jerk).

Fast forward six months later and a new CEO came in. The CIO seized the opportunity and had the CEO come in for a demonstration. He had coached us that the CEO's priorities were to be able to see what was happening in different stores without necessarily being in them, "just in time" merchandising, and manufacturing with Asia. Fifteen minutes into the demonstration the CEO said, "I want it, make it happen." He was a very High D. Thirty days later, with the same gentleman from Purchasing we had a deal at 17.5 percent discount. What was the difference? The value of the solution and the person we were doing business with. He understood getting the solution in ASAP was worth a lot more than negotiating a bigger discount that would have taken six months. We got a big deal and negotiated that we could use his stores as demo sites and his application as a case study.

In all instances, once you choose one strategy, the other strategies will become tactics you use throughout the negotiation, especially in the Give/Get and Bigger Picture. For example, you might give on something (play it Soft) but not on another (Firm) while coming up with an alternative offer on something else (Give/Get).

A GOOD NEGOTIATION STRUCTURE

Regardless of your strategy, the following negotiation structure helps maintain a high standard of quality and consistency when you are actually negotiating:

1. Preparing for the negotiation
2. Setting the stage, tone, and intent
3. Asking and understanding any concerns or issues
4. Discussing and coming to closure and agreement on these issues

Preparing for the Negotiation

Going into a negotiation without preparation is like competing in a sporting event without anticipating what your competitor will do. The negotiation form in the appendix will help you prepare.

Setting the Stage, Tone, and Intent

Setting the tone for a negotiation can begin in a positive or an ominous way. Regardless of your strategy, you should establish that you want both parties to come out of the negotiation feeling like they are getting what they want, even if it is only a one-time transaction. Even somebody who only buys from you once can be a reference or can tell other people to buy from you.

The way I like to set the tone for a negotiation is to tell people that I am happy that we are at this stage, that it is my job to be mindful of all the things that have brought us here, and we will know we have negotiated successfully if we are happy at the end of it. I also like to remind them that we will probably come up against issues that we disagree with, but those shouldn't cause us to lose sight of what we both want and what has brought us together. This gives people a chance to respond in kind, to let me see if they react well or go into hysterical laughter at my naiveté.

Another way to start is to begin summarizing all the things you know, have done, they have told you, etc. then get their thoughts and ask them if they agree or if they have any questions, issues, or concerns. You might also consider having the negotiation happen in a neutral place that in itself creates a better setting and tone for the negotiation. If you can help it, never negotiate via e-mail. Conversely, if the prospect is physically close enough, or the deal is big enough, try to do as much of the negotiation as possible in person.

Asking about and Positioning Questions, Concerns, or Issues

The simplest way to determine if prospects have any questions, concerns, or issues is to ask (some people don't like to use the word *concerns* or *issues* and replace it with *questions,* which is fine). If they don't, close them and go out and buy a lottery ticket, because this is your lucky day. If they do, write them down or, if you can, list them on a board or somewhere you can both see them. I have done this on a paper placemat (not linen) in a restaurant or during a web conferencing session on a virtual whiteboard. Then, ask them if there are any others and if you can address these, would they be willing to sign a contract, move ahead, do business, etc. This is critical for several reasons, including:

- You now know what you have to do to win the business and have positioned them against the sale.
- If they come back afterwards and tell you there are additional issues, you can tell them everything you had negotiated prior is off the table.
- You can do a Give/Get with their own issues (in fact you can ask them which ones are most important to get from you).

Discussing and Coming to Closure and Agreement on Negotiation Issues

Once you know their issues, ask them to prioritize them. You might, depending on how strong a position you are in, write down any concerns or issues you have. I like to address the issues I know I can handle easiest and/or I know I can give them something. Why? Because when I get to the ones I cannot handle, I can play off what I have already given them and am in a better position. Here is a simplified example where a salesperson knows she is in short supply of a certain product:

Prospect: "My biggest issues are price, delivery, and service."
Salesperson: "OK, thanks for your honesty. Do you have any others?"
Prospect: "No."
Salesperson: "Great. If you don't mind me asking, because I know your concerns, can you tell me what you like about our offer that brought us together?"
Prospect: "I love your functionality, the looks of your product, and I have heard great things from my friends."
Salesperson: "Wonderful. I am happy to hear that. So let's discuss your concern about our prices. Can you tell me more?" (Did you notice the salesperson acknowledged and asked a question?)
Prospect: "Sure. You are asking for way too much."
Salesperson: "OK, if you don't mind, can you be a bit more specific?" (Another question.)
Prospect: "The upfront fee is way too much. I don't like to pay anything until I see how it performs."
Salesperson: "Is that your only concern regarding the price?" (A third question.)
Prospect: "Yes."
Salesperson: "The fee is structured that way so we can provide the services you want, but I think I can do something about that depending on the rest of our conversation. Please tell me about your service concern."

Prospect: "Well, we are in a remote area and I don't see how you could get somebody out to fix it if it breaks."

Salesperson: "And you are worried it will break at the worst possible time" (anticipating the objection).

Prospect: "Exactly."

Salesperson: "Anything else?" (Another question, but a good one.)

Prospect: "That is it."

Salesperson: "I can't imagine this is the first time you have encountered this problem. What have others done for you?"

Prospect: "Any number of things."

Salesperson: "We have an overnight cross-shipping program where you send us the broken unit and we send you a new one so you are never out for more than one day. We also have a program where you can stock the most critical parts and we can walk you through how to fix it. Would either of those suffice?"

Prospect: "Yes."

Salesperson: "Great. Now tell me about your concerns around delivery."

Prospect: "Well we really need to get started in fifteen days and you said your standard was thirty."

Salesperson: "May I ask if you have prepared everything so you can use it in fifteen days, including getting rid of your old system and being trained?"

Prospect: "We assumed you would take the old system and we could do the training beforehand."

Salesperson: "Those are both possible, but we don't like to do the training until you have the system or you will forget stuff. We have a few choices: (1) we can get it to you sooner and schedule your training, but there is an additional charge; (2) I can give you a loaner at a nominal rate; or (3) if you want me to get it to you sooner, I may not be able to give you the price reduction you asked for (giving and getting with their own issues). Which of these is most appealing?"

This example is a fair representation of a negotiation that is done by two parties who respect each other and want to come to an amicable resolution. When we get to the session involving tactics, you will see that people don't always negotiate this way and make things much more difficult.

THERE IS NO SUCH THING AS A NEGOTIATION ISSUE

When I teach my classes, I tell everyone that I will give them twenty dollars if they can give me a negotiation issue, resistance, or concern that I can't deal with as an objection. I do this because it is true and to give them confidence that they can handle "issues" like they handle objections. It is also an easy way for me to win twenty dollars. Let's list some issues and see if they can be categorized and handled as objections. (I will only show you Steps 2 and 3 of the Five-Step Objection Handling Process):

Issue	Handle as Objection
Too expensive	Thanks for your honesty. (Acknowledge.) Can you tell me more about your concern? (Question.)
Have to think about it	This is an important decision. (Acknowledge.) Is there anything in particular you are unsure of? (Question.)
Have to see what others think	Everyone needs to be happy. (Acknowledge.) What are you looking for them to say? (Question.)
Concerned about your terms and conditions	We both need to be happy. (Acknowledge.) Please tell me more. What in particular are your concerns? (Question.)
Can't meet their delivery schedule	Thanks for your candor. (Acknowledge.) Other than that, are you happy with our solution? Tell me about your concern? (Questions.)
Want a better guarantee	OK. (a short acknowledgment) What about our current guarantee makes you uncomfortable? (Question.)
Need certain functionality you don't have	It needs to do what you want. (Acknowledge.) Besides the functions you want, do we have most of what you have? Tell me what we don't have and let's see if we can find a way to make this work. (questions)

HANDLING TACTICS

In negotiations, there are many tactics that you can use or may be used against you. These can be fair, harsh, or somewhere in between, depending on the DiSC style of the person, their job responsibilities, the pressure people are under, the strategy of the parties involved, and the seriousness of the outcomes. Below are examples of how to handle the most common and/or difficult:

Tactic: Ridiculously low offer.
Counter: Ridiculously high offer, change your offer, walk away/call their bluff, wince in shock of disappointment.
Tactic: Used-car tactic (tell you they have to talk to their boss or someone else).
Counter: Have all parties in same room at same time.
Tell them you want to negotiate with their boss.
Refuse to negotiate this way.

Do the same thing with them.

Tactic: Reduce size of deal or take only less expensive components (which makes it less profitable).

Counter: Reduce the offer, start from the beginning (you can prevent this by having your proposals say that any change to any item in the proposal is a change to the entire proposal), don't line-item the prices of your proposals.

Tactic: Change negotiator.

Counter: You do same.

Do S.PRI.N.G. Dialogue before you do anything.

Take your time setting up appointment to put some time pressure on them.

Tactic: Nibbling, constantly asking for more.

Counter: Tell them it changes everything.

Say "no," politely.

Start nibbling back telling them you want more or have to take back what you have already given.

Tactic: You need us more than we need you (usually when the customer is very big).

Counter: Isolate the negotiation only to the deal and not what comes after it. Take away their size by doing this. Have a lot in your funnel so you don't need their business. If negotiating with Purchasing, see if the businessperson can influence.

Tactic: The prospect doesn't return your calls or e-mails to resume discussion.

Counter: Go over the head of the person you are talking to. If it is Procurement, let the businessperson who wants you know so they can put some pressure on Procurement to respond, tell them that the offer expires at a certain time (this should also be on all of your proposals). Take your time responding to them when they do respond.

Tactic: Downplay your advantages, "commoditize" you, or tell you they can go with someone else.

Counter: Call their bluff, remind them of your advantages and differences, ask why they are even talking to you if they feel that way. Have a comparison chart that outlines the differences and benefits to them.

Tactic: They say they have a better offer price-wise, or their budget is limited.

Counter: Ask, in a polite way, for them to prove it by showing you either. Tell them you can match the price if you get a bigger order. Remind them of the differences and benefits that would be worth more than if they got it from the other vendor for free. Offer financing versus a straight purchase. Have them start with a smaller deal.

Tactic: They say their budget is limited.

Counter: Ask, in a polite way for them to prove it. Remind them of the differences and benefits. Offer financing versus a straight purchase. Have them start with a smaller deal. Ask them how important buying your offer is versus others and ask them to take money away from the less important purchases.

If you are experiencing many or more tactics than these in a single situation, then you are either dealing with a very thorough and professional negotiator or with someone who doesn't care about your offer. In either instance, you should stop the negotiation and consider whether you want to continue.

TEAM NEGOTIATIONS

All too often, people try to negotiate deals alone. There are many reasons you shouldn't do this, but they all tend to boil down to the idea that four, six, or eight eyes or ears are better than two. Also, different people on your side can have more authority when negotiating certain issues. Here are some reasons or triggers where you might want to bring someone else with you:

- You just aren't getting along with the person with whom you are negotiating.
- The negotiation is stuck.
- You are negotiating with someone older, younger, or of a different gender; and although no one is saying so, you know it is getting in the way.
- The deal is of a certain complexity or size that you have never dealt with.
- Language or cultural issues.
- Legal and financial issues that are beyond your responsibility.
- You are negotiating with someone who has a much bigger title than you, and she wants to negotiate with someone with a similar title.

R.E.A.L. TIPS AND REMINDERS

- ☑ You are usually in a stronger position than you think, or the prospect wants you to know.
- ☑ Always get all issues on the table when negotiating.
- ☑ Don't get emotional or take things personally.
- ☑ If you have to give, try to give in small increments things of high value to the client and low cost to you.
- ☑ Always anticipate issues before you go into a negotiation.
- ☑ The better your pipeline, the better negotiator you will be.
- ☑ Negotiate to satisfy business and personal issues and needs.
- ☑ You usually have more in common with the prospect than less; you just forget.
- ☑ Try not to give without getting.
- ☑ Know your bottom line or alternative offer before negotiating.
- ☑ Most, if not all issues, objections, and resistance are really objections—treat them as such.

☑ Never negotiate over e-mail. If a customer raises an issue, tell him you would like to speak about it and set a time to do so.

☑ The more T.E.E.M. people give to a negotiation, the harder it is for them to walk away. Don't be afraid to add a little of your own time in responding or ask the prospect to do a little something to add up T.E.E.M. points.

☑ If they are not nice people and you see they are very win/lose type of negotiators, any time they bring up an issue say, "That may be difficult."

☑ A series of concessions, no matter how minor, creates an environment of superiority/inferiority in a negotiation. Be aware if this is happening to you. Professional negotiators will try and do this to you.

☑ If they say they are giving you the deal (but have changed the proposal you have offered) tell them they are changing the terms and need to negotiate around the new things they are asking for.

☑ Negotiate the financial value of your solution in relation to their priorities when they tell you your solution is too expensive. Know what it would cost them if they don't go with you.

☑ If they ask you to reduce price, ask them what you should take out of the proposal.

☑ Take a strategic view of your assignment/quarterly goals and know which ones you will and won't give in to.

☑ You can change negotiators to substantiate a point or if you are stalled or if they change personnel.

☑ Whenever you meet someone in a negotiation, do a S.PRI.N.G. Dialogue, especially with Procurement. You want to know what else is important to them besides price (Turnaround time of orders, customer satisfaction, etc.).

☑ You can ask for a time-out in any negotiation if you need time to get your head straight or think about something.

11

Putting and Keeping It All Together

S.M.A.R.T. GOALS, PRIORITIES, AND TIME MANAGEMENT

The one thing every entrepreneur, businessperson, or salesperson has in common is time, how well or poorly they utilize it, and wishing they had more of it. Knowing where the best return for your time investment lies can be a real struggle because so many things might seem important, especially if you are just starting a business and have very little or no help.

But a funny thing happens if you are an entrepreneur: Work is not a burden but a calling—a passion—and you don't mind investing as much time as needed to be successful. In fact, you want to invest the time. But you still need to be smart about it so you can get the best from your effort. What if instead of wasting an hour a day, you could get one more hour a day back? That would be 240 more hours a year (5 days x 48 weeks=240 days or hours) which is about twenty-four more days (working ten hours a day) or about five more weeks. What would you do with five more weeks of time?

THE MACRO AND MICRO OF TIME MANAGEMENT

I think of goals and priorities as the macro part of effective time management, as the supporting structure in which things are done. The micro part is time management skills: being organized, handling administrative tasks well, etc. Both are discussed in this chapter.

In my view, a goal is the end result you want to achieve, a reflection of your passion and why you are an entrepreneur or salesperson, and priorities are the most important things that need to be done to attain the goal. Goals and priorities often look alike, so people sometimes confuse these, and it distracts them from the end goal. For example, a person might say his goal is to sell to his top five prospects while his real goal is to make a certain amount of money, which would be achieved in part by selling to his top five prospects. If he believes selling to the top five prospects is all he needs to do, he might miss other priorities that need to be executed (such as to upsell his customers or sell more service programs that have very high margins).

What is a S.M.A.R.T. Goal?

Specific: You need to be able to measure your progress as you work toward your goal. The more specific, the easier it is to achieve. Use numbers or percentages as a way of quantifying your goal.

Measurable: Make sure you can measure (qualitatively and quantitatively) how well you are doing against the specifics of the goal you set.

Aligned/Agreed Upon: Ensure goals are aligned and agreed upon with the people you need to support you inside and outside the company. This is often the hardest part but most critical.

Realistic (and aggressive): Goals must be realistic, taking into consideration such factors as how much time it takes, if needed resources are available, whether you have proper funding, the state of the economy, if you are doing other things (inside and outside of work), and other things that will prevent you from achieving this goal.

Timed: It is important to set a start and stop or beginning and end for your goal and your priorities. A time line keeps you focused, prevents procrastination, and keeps you accountable to yourself and others.

A few examples of well-written S.M.A.R.T. goals are:

- "I will make $200,000 in the next twelve months."
- "I will make 120 percent of my quota each month next year."
- "I will grow my business 25 percent over last year."
- "I will reduce expenses by 25 percent to address the recession and maintain at least 80 percent of last year's sales."
- "I will grow my business 25 percent and increase margins 10 percent over last year."

Priorities that need to be defined and executed to achieve the goal might be:

- Define the best prospects and accounts to sell to.
- Drop unprofitable accounts.
- Reduce overhead by 15 percent.
- Bring in systems and technology that will make people more productive and eliminate three new hires.

S.M.A.R.T. Goal Stories

Story 1

Many years ago I worked for a company that sold PCs to businesses. It was the first company to load the software onto the PC. Prior to that, businesses had to do it themselves. Needless to say, our sales were thriving. Unfortunately, our support and service were not keeping up. My boss, a charismatic leader who abhorred detail, recognized the only way to fix this was to have a meeting every morning at 7:30 AM for one hour, with all the different departments represented—purchasing, tech support, sales, information technology, shipping, and others. The goal was to have all orders go out within three days of receipt with a 99 percent out-of-box reliability (the "S" in S.M.A.R.T.). The priorities were to fix the work flow from beginning to end by going over every order (which helped us get PCs to clients) and to develop the proper processes to meet our ninety-day sales goal.

Nobody wanted to do this. It was hard work, but because he was a great leader, it actually became something people looked forward to. Doughnuts, coffee, rewards, etc. were all part of the process, and we achieved our ninety-day goal. Every quarter after that, he revisited the process to see if it was still working or there were ways to improve upon it.

Story 2

I was Senior Director of the northeast region and my team had been the top-performing team in the world for four years in a row. Because of this, the company chose to increase our quota by 80 percent and simultaneously drop the average sales price. Effectively our quota had increased 100 percent. Our compensation for this Herculean task was the same as the previous year. Finally, because we were in the Northeast, a decision had been made that we could achieve this without additional support people like administrators and secretaries.

You can imagine how motivated and excited we were (not). I went to my mentor at the time and asked him for advice, and he helped me turn this situation into the most valuable and rewarding of my career. For three days, my management team and key contributors from the region and our headquarters (they needed to be part of the process so they were aligned with what we were doing) went to an off-site location and decided on our goal (which was to be 110 percent of quota) and to break down the priorities of each position in the region. We went through a series of exercises to do this, which you will see later in this chapter. The first ninety days were very difficult, because we were doing something new and uncomfortable. However, because we had the all the right people there, were committed to our goal, and kept each other accountable, we ended up at 109 percent of quota.

I decided to leave at the top of my game to start IPG. Nonetheless, the region, because of the process, maintained its high productivity and position for the next two quarters without my replacement. That is how strong this process can be. My replacement told me it was the easiest transition he had ever made.

Choosing Your Goals and Priorities

Goal setting is exciting and energizing. It is proclaiming why you are an entrepreneur. It requires specificity and structure to guide you effectively. When I started my business in 1994, I had to:

- Decide my goal (notice I did not say goals, which would have distracted me and been too much to handle).

- Decide the most important things (priorities) for me to do to reach my goal.
- Test how much I really wanted to be in my own business.

For my business, I had to understand why I wanted to start my sales training business. What were the motivations behind my desire? What did the outcome look like from all perspectives (business, personally, family)? Was it an overreaction to a bad experience at the company I was working for or a real desire?

For me, the motivation was to be more independent. Specifically I did not want to work inside a company bureaucracy. I also wanted to do something I loved (which was to teach).

My motivation was also to have more time to do my yoga and develop that aspect of myself (which I have not achieved yet). Financially, I wanted to be able to retire by a certain age (if I so desired) and to have enough money to provide for my kids' education, weddings, etc.

Do you know the answers to these questions and others that are relevant for you? If not, give it some time to help you in this process.

Goal setting was the "easy" part compared to choosing my priorities. Setting priorities was more difficult because there were so many to choose from. I had no real experience to filter them. Additionally, I found that there were some priorities I just didn't want to do. For example, I had to decide if I was willing to travel more and be away from my kids. I had to decide if I was willing to spend my own money or not. I realized I needed to travel more than I had thought to start my business.

You may struggle with things you are not willing to do (which shows your desire to be successful), but it can also mean that your plan is not addressing the "R" or realistic part of S.M.A.R.T. goals. Just make sure you are being realistic, or it could come back to bite you and jeopardize everything you had hoped for.

Here are some exercises that helped me, and will help you, gain clarity. Be as specific as possible when you are doing them. Avoid general statements like "I am willing to work harder," and replace them with things like, "I am willing to work twelve hours a day." This exercise will also yield some things that may become priorities.

Prioritization Exercise

Willing to Do/Not Willing to Do: Write down anything and everything you can think of that you are willing or not willing to do. (See Table 11.1 for an example.)

Continue/Start/Stop: This is a good exercise to delineate anything you should continue or do more of, start doing, or stop/defer doing to help you get to your goals and define your priorities. If this is a brand-new venture, you will probably have more in the Start and Stop section

Table 11.1
Willing/Not Willing Priority-Setting Exercise

Willing to Do	Not Willing to Do
Work 12 hours a day	Work on Sundays
Spend 10% of my own money on marketing	Not see my girls
	Take money from the kids' education fund

because you don't know what to Continue or Do More Of (a way to address this is find a mentor or ask others who have been successful before you). Do this by yourself and then with others that are critical to your success. In part, this tests the "A" or Agreed/Aligned element of S.M.A.R.T. goals.). Table 11.2 provides an example of this exercise.

Other Priorities: Brainstorm with yourself or others the myriad number of possible priorities that might be critical to your success. The rules of brainstorming are to throw out any and all ideas and write them down. No explaining or justifying. They can be as far-fetched and extreme as possible. After you have run out of ideas, you can start deciding and discussing which ones are the most important. My sister taught me that a good way to do this is to go to opposite extremes. For example, if I say a priority might be to travel to Silicon Valley because there are a lot of prospects there, the opposite might be find all the similar prospects within a fifty-mile driving range of home (fortunately or unfortunately I never did that exact one so I have a lot of air mile points but am not home as much as I should be).

Table 11.3 is an example of how to set and define a S.M.A.R.T. business goal.

Table 11.2
Continue/Start/Stop Priority-Setting Exercise

Continue/Do More	Start	Stop/Defer
Building a list of people I will call to tell about my new sales training business.	Spending an hour a day to learn about the industry. Waking up an hour earlier every day.	Wasting time in the morning on things unrelated to starting my business (browsing the web or pursuing a personal hobby).

Table 11.3
S.M.A.R.T. Goal—To Make $250,000 in the Next 12 Months

Steps and Priorities	What I'll Do	Where/What Situation	How Many Hours per Week	When I Will Start and Complete	Resources Needed (people, info, money)	What Others Need to Do/$$
Meet with Top Accounts	Physically meet each	In their facility	5 per week	ASAP	Sales person and Customer Service	See if others can go on calls
Work with Customer Service	Discuss top accounts and prospects	In office at 8 AM	Every day for 30 minutes	July 1–Sept 30	Database, sales, customer support reps	Prepare reports for daily meetings
Get Mailing List	Buy e-mail list and send message to 50 people every week	n/a	2	Sept 1–Nov 30	Mailing list	$5,000 for list and admin to send out mailing

Figure 11.1
Sample of TAP'ing Your Weekly Time Calendar

Time	Mon	Tues	Wed	Thurs	Fri
7AM	Admin and email				
8	Strategize big deals	Team Meetings	1:1's	1:1's	1:1's
9	Customer Interactions and Meetings				
10					
11					
12PM					
1	Eat, Check email and vmail				
2	Customer Interactions and Meetings				
3					
4	OPEN	OPEN	OPEN	OPEN	OPEN
5	Call Key Cust.	Strategize big deals	Train Team	Call Key Cust	Prepare next week
6	Check email and vmail				

Once you establish your priorities, you put them into your calendar. I call these time-activated priorities (TAP). An example is shown in Figure 11.1.

GETTING OUT OF E-MAIL AND VOICEMAIL JAIL

More, if not most communications in today's business world are via voicemail, e-mail, text messaging, and other varieties of digital communications. And it can become very addictive because it gives you the false feeling you are busy and productive. It also feeds our need as human beings to connect, even if it is electronically. But for it to be effective, you must have a way of dealing with this so it doesn't interrupt you and become counterproductive. Knowing your S.M.A.R.T. goals and priorities is one of the most effective ways because it gives you a filter to decide which messages you should or should not respond to. If an e-mail or voicemail or text message doesn't directly relate, try not to respond. You are wasting your precious time.

In the story I told about when I was Senior Director of the northeastern region, I was getting burned out. We were working hard and I needed a vacation before the fourth-quarter push. I alerted everyone on my voicemail and e-mail that I was gone, was not taking messages, and not to leave me one because I couldn't do anything about it while I was away. When I got back, my voicemail box was full (over 150 voicemails) and I had over five hundred e-mails (which I think today would probably be about five thousand). My vacation had worked, and I was relaxed and didn't want to deal with all of the messages so I deleted them all. To this day, I don't know of one negative consequence of doing so. People solved their problem or got their question answered without me, or, it wasn't that important in the first place. I realized that my getting involved and reacting to all the messages left for me was just making it worse. From that day on, my attitude and approach have been different. I only respond to messages that directly relate to my goal and priorities. Of course normal priorities include things like responding to your boss, customers, and prospects if nobody else is better suited.

Here are several techniques that may be helpful in getting out of e-mail and voicemail jail.

- If possible, use technology to help handle your various messaging. Unified communication technology can put all your messages in one format and location so they are easier to handle.
- Use a PDA or other device to be responsive, but don't let it interfere with your goal and priorities.
- Use e-mail filters to weed out junk mail.
- Leave messages on your voicemail and e-mail when you will or won't be available for people to have the correct expectations.
- Turn your e-mail and phone off when you are involved in a priority project.
- Let people know how to contact you in case of emergency.
- Set aside specific times of the day when you will respond to your messages, except emergencies.
- Some companies have rules about hours that messages can be sent internally to avoid the overload.
- Create a protocol of when you should be involved in the e-mail chain (i.e., anything you are cc'd on does not require a response by you).
- There are companies that will automate how e-mail is handled to be more efficient.

Time Management on a Micro Level

There are probably more books written on time management than there are stars in the sky (well not that many, but a lot). At the time this book is being written there are 16,500,000 entries for the term *time management* in Google. Feel free to find the best ones for you.

Here are some questions to ask yourself about your own time-management habits that could be of assistance in figuring out where you need help (in case you're wondering, the right answer in each case is "yes"):

- Do you check e-mails at predesignated times versus reacting to each one as it comes?

- Do you "batch" certain administrative functions (paperwork, quotes, proposals) and do them all at once or do you do them as they are requested?
- Do you qualify requests from customers, prospects, and co-workers regarding when they need something versus just jumping at the request?
- Do you leave a voice/e-mail message letting people know when you are or are not available?
- Do you delegate and follow up many tasks versus doing them all yourself? Do you know which tasks should be ignored?
- Do your customers know the right people to contact for different needs versus coming to you for everything?
- Do you have one system where you keep notes, to-dos, etc.?
- Are you good at multitasking (e.g., checking e-mails and talking on phone)?
- If your job requires it, do you type well?
- Do you know how to operate the software packages and internal systems your computer uses well?
- Do you procrastinate and push off the lengthy or difficult tasks (even though they may be the most important)?
- Are you good at handling all the different paperwork that comes your way?
- Have you done everything you can to automate and remove as much paperwork as possible?
- In working your territory, do you try to make multiple appointments in the same area at the same time so you don't have to waste time traveling back and forth?
- Do you too often browse the web on unrelated work items?
- Do you gossip or spend too much time socializing during work hours?
- Do you qualify appointments as to whether you can do them on the phone versus in person?
- Do you qualify internal appointments as to whether you should attend or not?
- Do you use your selling hours to sell and do nonsales tasks at the appropriate time?
- Do you plan and prioritize the events for each day or week ahead of time and try to keep to it as much as possible?
- Do you set proper expectations with everyone as to when you will respond to people or do you just do whatever they ask whenever they ask?
- Do you come into work early enough knowing what you need to do (or do you come in too late and waste time getting organized)?
- Do you smoke so you have to go outside and waste time? (Here, the right answer is not "yes." Besides, in case you haven't heard, smoking is not healthy for you.)

Stephen Covey in his wonderful book *The 7 Habits of Highly Effective People* takes a unique perspective and suggests that people should identify the different roles others play in their lives (parents, entrepreneur, sibling, etc.) and define the priorities in each and put them into a weekly time calendar.

Some additional items that can help with time management are:

- Learn to say "no" to things that are not important.
- Don't be a perfectionist or do something in a rush so you have to do it again.
- TAP (time-activated priorities) in your weekly calendar. You are less likely to forget them.
- Make time in your calendar for the unexpected. If you don't you will get thrown off course more often and have a harder time achieving your goal and priorities.
- Don't reinvent the wheel every time. Create presentation and proposal templates that are quick and easy and can be easily modified to reflect your unique value.

AVOIDING THE EMOTIONAL ROLLER COASTER

Sales and selling is the greatest job in the world when you are doing well. You have a tremendous amount of freedom, meet good people, exude confidence, make lots of money, help people, are more selective about what business opportunities you engage in, become a better negotiator, and more. All the stars are in alignment. You are on a high, in sales ecstasy.

And it can all come tumbling down faster than you can imagine, which can be devastating. You can become desperate, anxious, have low self-esteem, worry a lot, become tentative and exhibit bad habits, chase bad business, and more. You lie awake at night worrying. Your prospects can "smell" your desperation and will take advantage of you without mercy.

It is essential that you not get too high or "full of yourself" when things are good or too low and lose your confidence when things are bad. Even the greatest athletes have slumps—and so do great salespeople.

Dealing with rejection is probably the most important part of keeping your emotional balance. As was discussed in the chapter on closing, if you close 40 percent of your deals, you are a superstar, but that means you didn't close 60 percent. Rejection comes in all sizes from a person not returning your call, to a person hanging up on you when you are prospecting, to a customer (even a happy one) not returning your calls, or saying "no" to some ideas you think are wonderful. And of course the ultimate rejection is losing a sale or several sales. The expression, "Don't take it personally, it is only business" is one I have abhorred for many years and personally have difficulty with. However, if you can embrace this, you will be much better off. And remember that most people will do first what serves them or their company best, and if you fit into that, great. And if not, well ...

I recently negotiated a deal with a very good customer in which I felt I wasn't being given the respect I deserved. It was a deal where the better they did, the more I got paid. The worse they did, the less I got paid. But the spirit of it turned, and it seemed my upside was much less than the risk

I was taking on the downside. When I presented this to them, it didn't really matter. I was afraid to pull out of the deal because of the impact it might have on other business we were doing. There are many lessons in this, but an important one is to deal with what is, be grateful for what you are given, and move on. Easier said than done, but there it is.

In another instance, a very good customer (not a prospect) would cancel appointments with no notice or apology. After five times I wrote her an e-mail saying I wish I got paid on the number of appointments she cancels or doesn't show up for versus the training I do for her. That didn't go over so well, but it is an example of where I should not have taken it personally. I should have bit my tongue, left my ego at the door, and just let it be.

Perhaps the most dramatic example is this: My main contact at a customer I had for five years, and whom I had actually counseled through some difficult personal and work issues, never told me when the company was considering another training alternative. He was a very High S, afraid of conflict, and more loyal to his company then me.

Please don't get the picture that all people are like this. Most aren't. The more successful you are at following the principles in this book, the more positive stories of loyalty and caring you will have. I have chosen these stories to paint a real picture of dealing with rejection and not letting it be too disruptive. My thirty-two years in sales and fourteen years as an entrepreneur have shown the best and worst sides of me, so here are some suggestions, things I have experienced myself, to help you maintain your confidence and avoid the roller coaster:

- Don't be underfunded.
- Hire the best.
- Prospect constantly.
- Keep to your Sweet Spot.
- Set realistic expectations.
- Stay balanced.
- Don't get greedy.
- Hire others to do things you don't like to do.
- Leverage existing customers for references.
- Focus on revenues.
- Develop partnerships.
- Keep costs down.
- Know yourself, your strengths, and limitations.
- Learn how to deal with stress.
- Keep your relationships strong.

To elaborate on some of the more important:

Don't go into your entrepreneurial venture underfunded. You will start out under pressure and that is not good. Know how much you have to spend and for how long. Write a business plan to help you do this. I did this well, and it allowed me to set proper expectations for myself and my family.

Hire and pay the best people you can. They always perform and are worth the extra they ask for.

Constantly market and prospect so you constantly have a full funnel. This is essential. Never stop. I tell my students their epitaph should say "I died prospecting."

Prospect and market to your Sweet Spot so you get a better return on your investment of time and money. Don't set unrealistic expectations of yourself. Have quarterly plans that are ambitious but realistic.

Stay balanced in your life. Don't make work your only thing because you will eventually burn out. Work hard but work out, have a social life, etc. Don't be greedy (despite what Michael Douglas says in the movie *Wall Street*). A piece of something is better than nothing of something big.

Hire people to do the things you don't want or like to do, even in the beginning (thus the need for ample funding). If you can't afford to, decide on your top three to four priorities and stick to them. Don't take on too much. Less is more if you have chosen the right priorities.

Once you have them, leverage your customers for references so you can get easier sales. Develop strong partnerships that can give you leads and advice.

Know your emotional, psychological, and financial limits before you start and keep to them. Being burned out is a sure way to fail. If you are having difficulties dealing with stress, see a doctor or homeopathic healer to see if they can help. Pray, chant, meditate, do yoga, exercise, knit, run, etc. to relieve the stress, then work hard, pray, chant, do yoga, exercise, knit, run to relieve the stress, then work hard.

If you are in a relationship you care about, do your best not to ruin or erode it while you are working so hard. It's easy to get too focused on your work.

Whatever you have to do, keep your confidence up. Starting anything new is difficult and takes time. Sales is all about avoiding the roller coaster of good and bad times.

R.E.A.L. TIPS AND REMINDERS

- ☑ Focus on S.M.A.R.T. goals.
- ☑ Prioritize and manage your time effectively.
- ☑ Stay out of voicemail and e-mail jail.
- ☑ Think about time on a macro and micro level.
- ☑ Avoid the emotional roller coaster.
- ☑ Don't get too stressed out.

Appendix

R.E.A.L.™* CREATING AND DEFINING YOUR SOLUTION

Priority	Feature/Function/ Service Product/ Offering	Operational/ Technical/ Functional Benefit	Business/Finan- cial Department Benefit	Individual and/or Company Benefit
Benefits in Summary				

*Relevant—Effective—Applied—Learning

R.E.A.L.™ PREMEETING ORGANIZER

What	Who	Notes
Prospect or existing customer		
Length of time with you and revenue if existing client?		
Why did they originally choose your company?		
How much revenue are we supporting?		
Any recent change in contacts?		
Current or previous programs		
Search Internet and website for current news and events about client		
Prepare questions you want to ask and things you want to accomplish		
Create agenda for meeting		
Confirm attendees and avoid no-show		
Any materials need to be sent to customer		
Communicate plan with your company attendees		
Anticipated pushback		
Room set-up		

R.E.A.L.™ PRESENTATION ORGANIZER

What	Who	Notes
Introduction of people, backgrounds, and responsibilities		
Opening line—gambit/ice breaker, finding things in common, tell them about themselves, their business, their history, why they started the company, why did they do it?, etc.		
Have the prospects introduce their people and their roles		
Give an overview of the agenda and ask prospect for confirmation, input, and any changes		
Ask what they want to have accomplished in the time together so they would feel comfortable buying into your company or to make the time as valuable as possible		
Review and confirm your understanding of their current situation and their desires, priorities, and needs (if S.PRI.N.G. was done before meeting)		
Present your corporate pitch with modifications to their world		
If relevant or appropriate, present the solution/top capabilities that are most relevant to the prospect and most unique to you		
Show your ROI and TTV (time-to-value)		
Provide references		
Q+A and summary that all subjects they were interested in were covered		
Define next steps		
Other:		
What objections will you get?		
What graphics will you use?		

R.E.A.L. Negotiation Planner

R.E.A.L.™ NEGOTIATION PLANNER

Key Contact

Title

Role in Decision

Personality Profile (DiSC)

Contact #2

Title

Role in Decision

Personality Profile (DiSC)

Describe Prospect's Current Environment:

Describe Competition:

Opportunity Size	Length of Commitment You Are Looking For	Product/s and Services Being Used/Proposed	Revenue Your Product Will Help Generate for Prospect

R.E.A.L.™ NEGOTIATION PLANNER

How will you begin the negotiation? (What is the key person's DiSC style, how strong is your relationship, do you want to position a Bigger Picture approach, do you need to ask their priorities, needs, gain, other):

How will you present or summarize their priorities and needs?

Key Priorities, Needs, Gain of Prospect (Business, Financial, Political/Personal, DiSC)	Benefits of Your Offer? What Is Unique That the Competition Can't Offer?	What Happens If They Don't Go with Your Company (business, Financial, Political/Personal, DiSC)

What Do You Anticipate Happening?

Objections/Issues/Concerns/Tactics	How Will You Respond? (what Questions Will You Ask before You Respond)?	Who Will Handle?

What Are You Willing to Give to Get What You Want?

Willing to Give for a Get Including Alternative Offers	Not Willing to Give (what is your bottom line)

What Will Be the Next Steps You Recommend If You Can't Close the Deal?

Index

About the Author

JONATHAN LONDON is President and Founder of the sales training consultancy Improved Performance Group, which has a blue-chip clientele. He has extensive experience in training and development in the areas of sales, leadership, and customer service. As a salesman or sales manager for corporations such as Olivetti, ROLM, Wyse/Amdek, NBI, and PictureTel, London earned numerous awards as the top producer in his company—or in the industry worldwide.